Praise for

A Woman of Strength and Purpose

"Wow! Cynthia Tobias has cracked the code for directing your passion and defining your purpose. Every strong-willed woman (not to mention the men who love them) needs to read this incredibly practical and insightful book."

> —DRS. LES AND LESLIE PARROTT, *New York Times*
> best-selling authors of *Saving Your Marriage Before
> It Starts*

"I thoroughly enjoyed *A Woman of Strength and Purpose.* I consider myself an SWW (strong-willed woman) and deeply appreciate Cynthia's take on how we can use our ambition and strength for God! The book provides real-life and modern-day stories of other strong women of faith that encouraged me and inspired me! It is a book that will motivate women of any age!"

> —MEGAN ALEXANDER, reporter for *Inside Edition*
> and author of *Faith in the Spotlight*

"Strong-willed women often struggle to know how their dynamic personalities fit with God's call. In this wise and insightful work, Cynthia Tobias has demonstrated that those two realities can work together beautifully! Indeed, strong-willed women can have a lasting and powerful impact on the world around them."

> —JIM DALY, president of Focus on the Family

"Thank you, Cynthia Tobias, for helping godly women understand that it's not only okay to be a confident woman with inner strength and purpose; it's God's design. This book is a great tool for women who desire to find the gentle balance between learning, leading, and loving others while following Christ."

—BABBIE MASON, award-winning recording artist, author, and songwriter

"Finally! A book that speaks to the many strong-willed Christian women in the world today. Along with real-life stories, Cynthia Tobias shares her expert and practical advice on how to celebrate, embrace, and use your God-given gift to honor Him. You'll be encouraged and uplifted as you learn how to be the best you can be in your relationships, work, and spiritual life."

—MARTHA HADLEY, Christian radio personality for the nationally syndicated *Martha Hadley Show*

"Strong, determined men tend to be celebrated in our Western culture. But that same culture often marginalizes, criticizes, and stigmatizes these same characteristics when they happen to be in a woman. Cynthia Tobias knows all about being a strong and determined woman. She also knows how to help you rise above the cultural pushback and purposefully leverage your strength for the greater good of the people you love and for the glory of the God who gave it to you."

—DR. TIM KIMMEL, best-selling author of *Grace-Based Parenting* and *Grace-Filled Marriage*

"I'm so glad Cynthia has written a book for us stronger-willed women. It took me a long time to accept the fact that God liked me. I knew He loved me because He says so, but like me? He also says He likes women of a quiet, gentle nature, and that just does not describe me. So this book touches a chord in me."

—GIGI GRAHAM, author and conference speaker

"Cynthia Tobias is the quintessential strong-willed woman. In her latest book, *A Woman of Strength and Purpose,* she gives her extraordinarily valuable insights into the personal challenges of women who have strong wills and those who love and/or work with them. It's rich information and great inspiration!"

—JAN SILVIOUS, author of *Fool-Proofing Your Life*
and *Big Girls Don't Whine*

"Have you ever been called a strong-willed woman? Maybe it was meant as a compliment—or maybe it wasn't. I can relate! For all of us strong women, Cynthia's message encourages us to embrace our strength—but to *always* direct that energy toward healthy goals and in a careful, godly way. Get ready: this book will excite, encourage, and challenge you."

—SHAUNTI FELDHAHN, social researcher and
best-selling author of *For Women Only*

"Cynthia Tobias's keen insights and stories will free your strong-willed mind, heart, and life. You'll discover how to live for Christ as you surrender your strong will to the One who rules the world and secures your place in it. This book will strengthen you to be the change-maker He designed you to be."

—PHYLLIS WALLACE, family counselor and former
radio host of *Woman to Woman*

"If you've ever struggled with whether God can make kingdom use of your strong-willed personality, *A Woman of Strength and Purpose* is your next read! Cynthia Tobias makes it crystal clear: a surrendered and consecrated strong will is an arrow in God's hand."

—ALLISON ALLEN, speaker, author, and actor

A WOMAN OF
STRENGTH
AND
Purpose

Cynthia Tobias
Prov 3:5-6

Books by Cynthia Ulrich Tobias

Nonfiction

*Every Child Can Succeed: Making the Most
of Your Child's Learning Style*

I Hate School! How to Help Your Child Love Learning

Middle School: The Inside Story

*The Way They Learn: How to Discover
and Teach to Your Child's Strengths*

*The Way We Work: A Practical Approach
for Dealing with People on the Job*

You Can't Make Me (But I Can Be Persuaded)

CYNTHIA ULRICH TOBIAS

A WOMAN OF
STRENGTH
AND
Purpose

Directing Your Strong Will to
• Improve Relationships
• Expand Influence
• Honor God

WATERBROOK

A WOMAN OF STRENGTH AND PURPOSE

Details in some anecdotes and stories have been changed to protect the identities of the persons involved.

Trade Paperback ISBN 978-1-60142-898-1
eBook ISBN 978-1-60142-897-4

Cover design by Kelly L. Howard

Published in the United States by WaterBrook, an imprint of the Crown Publishing Group, a division of Penguin Random House LLC, New York.

WATERBROOK® and its deer colophon are registered trademarks of Penguin Random House LLC.

Library of Congress Cataloging-in-Publication Data
Names: Tobias, Cynthia Ulrich, 1953– author.
Title: A woman of strength and purpose : directing your strong will to improve relationships, expand influence, and honor God / Cynthia Ulrich Tobias.
Description: First Edition. | Colorado Springs, Colorado : WaterBrook Press, 2016. | Includes bibliographical references.
Identifiers: LCCN 2016008488 (print) | LCCN 2016016931 (ebook) | ISBN 9781601428981 (trade pbk.) | ISBN 9781601428974 (electronic)
Subjects: LCSH: Christian women—Religious life. | Will—Religious aspects—Christianity.
Classification: LCC BV4527 .T623 2016 (print) | LCC BV4527 (ebook) | DDC 248.8/43—dc23
LC record available at https://lccn.loc.gov/2016008488

Printed in the United States of America
2016—First Edition

10 9 8 7 6 5 4 3 2 1

SPECIAL SALES
Most WaterBrook books are available at special quantity discounts when purchased in bulk by corporations, organizations, and special-interest groups. Custom imprinting or excerpting can also be done to fit special needs. For information, please e-mail special marketscms@penguinrandomhouse.com or call 1-800-603-7051.

TO MY **STRONG-WILLED** DAD, Robert Ulrich,
who taught me throughout my life how a strong will
that's surrendered to God can change the world.
Dad's life has been living proof of that,
and I'll forever be grateful for his example.

Contents

WHO SAYS I'M A
Strong-Willed
WOMAN?

Strong-Willed Woman. It's a galvanizing phrase. It evokes an immediate reaction—either positive or negative. There's no middle ground, no indifference. It's a term that is not neutral.

There are those who believe the term *strong willed* is automatically negative, describing a person who is stubborn, defiant, and difficult to deal with. But that's not the definition of strong will—that's what happens when strong will goes sideways. Strong will, in and of itself, is a positive trait; it describes a person who is energized, resourceful, and determined to succeed.

I am a strong-willed woman (SWW). I grew up the daughter of an evangelical pastor, and I never rebelled against my dad. I didn't talk back to a teacher or get loud, obnoxious, or rude. I tell people that you couldn't have traced even half the trouble I caused back to me! Outwardly I was compliant and cooperative. But if someone pointed a finger in my face, if someone told me something simply couldn't be done—that's when I dug in my heels and pushed back.

As I grew up, I had other strong-willed friends who were more independent, extroverted, and outspoken. Although some were unlike me in many ways, we all shared the same basic traits that make strong will such a positive force for good. We weren't afraid to tackle tough situations; we didn't back down just because circumstances were difficult. If we didn't know what to do, we figured out that someone in our network of friends and contacts would help us accomplish the goal. We excelled in finding creative alternatives.

During my first year of teaching high school, for instance, I was the girls' drill team faculty advisor. That meant getting forty high school girls to every football game. Unfortunately, I quickly found out that school bus drivers were scarce. Other people might just shrug, wring their hands, and say, "Well, that's just the way it is." But I thought, *How hard can it be to drive a bus?*

The next Sunday at church I pulled aside the Sunday school

director and pointed to the seventy-two-passenger school bus parked outside. "Pastor Bob, can someone teach me to drive that bus?"

He smiled. "I can make that happen."

In short order, I passed the driving test and got my special license—and my drill team girls had a reliably available school bus driver.

Because we quickly get a reputation as someone who can get the job done, SWWs tend to be called upon to figure out tough issues for other people too. All my life my family and friends have turned to me when they run into particularly hard situations: *There are no hotel rooms available. I can't find a rental car under sixty-five dollars a day. No one can figure out how to get there.* It's not that I have special skills; I just don't like taking no for an answer. I'm against giving up or admitting defeat when it's really important that something gets done.

Years ago, when I started traveling a lot for speaking engagements, the airlines had a rule that in order to get the best fares, you had to stay over a Saturday night. One weekend I was finished speaking at my event. Knowing that my young twins were both sick with colds, I decided I needed to head home even though it was still Saturday. I called the airline to see if I could get a flight out that night. The customer-service person informed me that the Saturday night stay could not be waived without great expense, and that I would have to wait until

Sunday morning. But I knew this airline had more than forty thousand employees, and every time I called the reservations number a different person answered the phone. I also knew there were several empty seats on that Saturday night flight, so I kept calling back until I found a reservation agent who would make the exception for me without penalty—and I got home to my sick kids on Saturday night.

SWWs are experts at finding loopholes, figuring out a way around a rule that doesn't make sense, or maneuvering around even the biggest obstacles. They are undaunted, undeterred, and sometimes succeed just through sheer perseverance.

But this book isn't talking about just *any* kind of strong-willed woman. Strong will has a dark side, and when it takes the wrong turn, things can get ugly. Resourcefulness can turn into manipulation; creative solutions can become dishonest tactics; determination can present itself as purely stubborn pride. Every strong-willed woman has experienced both the light and dark sides of her nature. We know we are capable of great good—or great destruction. The difference in how we use the power we have lies in whether or not we have dedicated it to the Creator and Designer of it.

When honoring God is our top priority, our greatest triumph is succeeding without cheating, being dishonest, or using any other tactic that would dishonor Him. As we're called upon to find unique solutions to problems or creative angles for attempting the impossible, we are fully committed to staying within the boundaries of God's law and direction and using our strong will to change the world for good. One woman put it this way: "A strong will doesn't have to have negative consequences, especially if it keeps us following in the footsteps God wants us to follow. It might be a lifesaver."

So what do we mean by *strong-willed women*? If we were talking about an army, these women would qualify to be part of a special operations unit. Special ops members stand apart from the others, not necessarily because they are smarter or more gifted than those in the infantry, but because they are, quite simply, *bolder.* In God's army, we find strong-willed special ops women from all walks of life—teachers, stay-at-home moms, CEOs, cashiers, homeschooling moms, entrepreneurs, missionaries, neurosurgeons, mail carriers. Whatever they do, wherever they are, they meet the world head-on—unafraid, undaunted, undeterred by those who tell them something can't be done. Each one is a woman with convictions of steel, willing to take the lead when called upon to use her passion, courage, and drive to withstand extraordinary conditions—even when her commitment requires a seemingly impossible mission.

Today more than ever, we're in a battle between good and evil. There is an enemy who is determined to steal the hearts and minds of children, destroy marriages, crush ambitions, and redefine ethics and spiritual morality. This is no ordinary warfare, and the stakes are higher than temporary victory. The outcome of this warfare determines the destiny of every soul for eternity.

God doesn't force us to serve, but when we voluntarily enlist in His service, we become part of something greater than any of us, and He uses our strong will to accomplish more than we could have ever dreamed. As Paul reminded us in 1 Thessalonians 1:4–5: "It is clear to us, friends, that God not only loves you very much but also has put his hand on you for something special. When the Message we preached came to you, it wasn't just words. Something happened in you. The Holy Spirit put steel in your convictions." God gave us a strong will for a reason—and He calls us to use it for Him.

The Enemy would have us think that it's wrong to possess strong will. He tries to make us feel guilty for using it or to discourage us from speaking up, especially in the church. That's because he knows that when strong will is voluntarily given to God and used for His purposes, it becomes a mighty force for God. Can you imagine how quickly the Enemy has to flee when faced with groups of godly, strong-willed women coming together to pray? Do you think these women will be reluctant to step up and fight injustice, crime, or any other evil? Will they be afraid to stand against what's wrong or be daunted by seemingly impossible tasks? I don't think so.

We won't all be called to fight in the same way—some will be on the front lines; others will prefer to work in the background—but every SWW serving God will play a critical role in carrying out His mission.

HOW STRONG WILLED ARE YOU?

When it comes to identifying who is officially a strong-willed woman, you'll find a huge variety of strengths and character traits. While we have many things in common, none of us will ever fit into a typical profile and description. Every SWW is unique, with stories so diverse and life experiences so varied that sometimes the only thing we can count on is never being bored!

You may already be comfortable with your strong will, embracing it with enthusiasm, or you may be reluctant to admit you have it—and resist using the term at all. You may live using intuition and spontaneity, or you might rely more on analysis and predictability. Strong will comes in all sizes, shapes, and personalities. But regardless of your background or uniqueness, you can use your strength to bring honor and glory to God— and you're destined to change the world in ways you can't even imagine. After all, it's almost always the ones with the most determination who make the most difference.

Of course, there's no definitive test to determine who is and isn't strong willed, but the following checklist can give you a good idea of the degree of strong will you have. Since we often get a better perspective of ourselves through the eyes of those

How Strong Is Your Will?

Put a check mark in front of each of the following statements that best describes you.

____ 1. I can be very creative and resourceful when I need to accomplish a difficult goal.

____ 2. I'm not easily discouraged by circumstances if the goal is important to me.

____ 3. I'm willing to step up and take on a project when no one else will.

____ 4. I am not easily intimidated.

____ 5. I don't automatically take no for an answer.

____ 6. When given the ultimatum, "Do it or else," my first reaction is, "Or else what?"

____ 7. I usually become the leader in a group.

____ 8. If the rule doesn't make sense to me, I look for ways around it.

____ 9. I may resist unconditional obedience in order to offer a few terms of negotiation before complying.

who love us, ask at least two other people who know you best to take this same checklist on your behalf and see if *their* score for you matches your own. (If you're married, be sure one of those people is your husband.)

____ 10. I don't shy away from adventure or steps of faith if I really believe God has told me to do something.

____ 11. I've been told I don't apologize as quickly or as often as I should.

____ 12. When backed into a corner, I'm more likely to keep fighting than to just give up.

Total _____

If you scored between eight and twelve, you definitely qualify as a strong-willed woman! If you scored less than eight, you probably think that you really don't have all that much strong will, and yet, as you read through this book, you might be surprised how many times you recognize yourself. Even if you don't come out high on the strong-willed scale, you'll find this book contains a wealth of knowledge for how to bring out the best in the strong-willed women you know and love.

IT TAKES ONE TO KNOW ONE

You would expect the author of this book to be an SWW—and I am. But there's something I'd like to clear up right away. This book is not about me—not all about my story or my views or my accomplishments. The truth is, God called me to write this book. I know you may think that sounds a little over the top, but I've never been more sure about anything in my life.

I had to fight hard to put this book in your hands—and the battles were not with flesh and blood. They were, and continue to be, fought against the Enemy of our souls. I know what Paul wrote about when he warned, "We do not wrestle against flesh and blood, but against principalities, against powers, against the rulers of the darkness of this age, against spiritual hosts of wickedness in the heavenly places" (Ephesians 6:12, NKJV).

During the course of finding a home for this manuscript, some people told me: "You're not reaching a broad enough range of women—the audience for this subject is too narrow." My response? "I believe it's a lot bigger than you think." Many people will be surprised by how many other godly SWWs are out there. In fact, I recruited several hundred of them to share, through a series of surveys and conversations, their thoughts, their struggles, and their advice. Oh, how I have enjoyed spending more than a year reading and thinking about what they wrote! What a privilege it's been to pray for them by name and to trust God to provide the best way to weave their words into this book.

Throughout the following pages you'll read comments from some of the more than four hundred women who responded to my surveys—SWWs who have a heart for God. Their words are honest and unvarnished and offer intimate glimpses into the lives of those who struggle to keep their resolve firmly under the control of the God they love and trust.

If you've ever been accused of being too bossy, too controlling, too intense; if you've ever struggled with letting your husband lead or gone toe-to-toe with your stubborn child; if you've ever wondered why the skills that make you so good at your job don't work at all in personal relationships; if you often wonder why some people don't *just snap out of it,* you'll find encouraging and intriguing answers in the following chapters. It's important to know that many women think a lot like you do.

Welcome to a book that understands you, written by someone who gets who you are and how you're wired. No one who has contributed to this book will raise her eyebrows and say, "I can't believe you think like that!" You'll be *encouraged* as you recognize how positive your strong will is when it's pointed in the right direction. You'll feel *reaffirmed* as you discover how much you have in common with other women of such strength and purpose, and how "normal" you are. Most of all, you'll feel *challenged* as you identify the practical ways to use your gift of strong will to honor God and His purposes.

As you read these pages, you'll find insights and strategies for every relationship—from leadership to friendships to marriage to parenting to, most importantly, your relationship with God. You'll smile as you read the comments, confessions, and advice from others who have walked in your shoes. You'll nod a lot and find yourself thinking, *That's me!* You may feel like one woman who wrote: "My history with the phrase *strong willed* has the connotation of 'head butting' or disobedience or selfishness. Is there something wonderful about this word that I've been missing all these years?"

Yes—and you're about to find out what it is. Are you ready to start this adventure?

WE'RE ALL **DIFFERENT—**
YET SO *Alike!*

I was having a business lunch with my very strong and determined friend Jean, and we started talking about what we SWWs have in common. "One thing is for sure," I said. "We're wired to *take action*!"

She nodded. "Absolutely."

I stood. "That's right. So let's *go,* let's get it *done.*"

Jean shook her head, and with the same resolute tone I had used, she stated, "No. First, we sit down and figure out a *plan.*"

I frowned. "Sit and *plan*? *That's* not action!"

How can two women be so different and still share the common bond of strong will? There are certainly no labels or descriptions that capture the nuances and depths of what it means to *be* a woman of such strength and purpose—we're each wired with a unique combination of temperament, personality, and learning style. No one will be able to completely define or describe you, but in these pages you're bound to find familiar descriptions of some of the ways you think and feel, especially if you've always known you don't fit the traditional mold.

You'll also discover that most SWWs who seek to honor God don't spend much time comparing themselves to one another—they have better things to do with their time. Galatians 5:26 puts it this way: "We will not compare ourselves with each other as if one of us were better and another worse. We have far more interesting things to do with our lives. Each of us is an original."

Even with all our differences, what we have in common is much more compelling. When my survey asked, "What are you like when your strong will is at its best?" you can only imagine the variety of answers it sparked. Some of the same words and phrases were repeated over and over, however, regardless of other variables. The following is a list of the most common.

What Am I Like When My Strong Will Is at Its Best?

I am . . .

- willing to tackle what others say can't be done
- good at motivating others when they've lost hope
- willing to endure discomfort to hold my ground
- persistent
- able to speak up for the needs of others
- standing in the gap for the weak
- resourceful
- undaunted by circumstances
- determined to get things done
- creatively energizing those around me

We have a lot of good characteristics going for us. Here are a few more positive traits that SWWs have, regardless of how different our personalities are.

We Want to Leave the World Better Than We Found It

Every SWW, regardless of any number of unique characteristics, has the power and potential to become a significant force that changes the world. We aren't content simply to blend in with the crowd. We want to do something significant, something extraordinary—and we can't rest unless we feel we're pursuing that.

For many of us, that significance means seeking a life full of adventure and conquering as many challenges as possible. Inspiration and passion fuel the drive to achieve our goals. We can be champions of worthy causes, be strong for those who can't defend themselves, change a system that's failing, or boldly fight injustice.

For others, it may mean taking a less visible approach. For one of my SWW friends, it means working quietly in the background as she advocates for the less fortunate—the poor, the disadvantaged, the lost. She intensely dedicates her life to fundraising, organizing events, and working to provide care and services, especially for delinquent and troubled children.

Whether it's making a difference from the spotlight on the stage or behind the scenes, through open confrontation or quiet conflict resolution, every SWW knows in her heart that she *is* destined to make a difference. You may even be like Pam in Ohio, with a strong dose of both approaches:

I was born with a passionate nature and two competing inner voices: *quiet and agreeable* or *loud and opinionated.* So one of my strongest personal goals (many long years in the making) is always to take time and decide if something is important enough to speak up about, and if I think my

input will help the situation. If the answer is yes, then I try
to find my truly strong voice—one that is loud enough to
be taken seriously, but still gentle enough to be heard.

We Can't Just Stand There—We Have to Do Something!

For most of us, it's hard to imagine how we can truly make a
difference without causing at least *some* trouble and creating
inconvenience while we're doing it. After all, how can we change
the world if we're just like everyone else?

Lynda wanted to make a difference and knew the uniqueness of her strong will was exactly what she needed to do just
that.

I stretch a long way before I plant my feet, but when I do,
it takes a miracle the size of parting the Red Sea to uproot
them . . . and only God or a little child can do it. I am
usually energized and excited because I truly believe God
has "shown me the way." For example, it was uphill all the
way to start a "no cost" summer program for at-risk kids.
God gave me a believing, incredible crew, and after many
months, we bullied the city into letting us have access to
an abandoned school with nothing but our elbow grease
to fix it. City lawyers kept telling me "no way" and "what's
the point?" and tried to shut us down through various
permit requirements and city regulations.

But I planted my feet for the kiddos, and one day, I challenged the lawyers to take a lunch tour with me. I bought them McDonald's Happy Meals and drove past boarded-up, run-down houses where some of the kids lived. I shamed them into leaving the safety of their locked car, promising them I'd be their five-foot-two-inch bodyguard, and began knocking on doors to shake hands with a few of the families still living in those "vacated" houses. Most of those young kids walked eight miles down a bustling one-way city street every day to get to our program. Before I even turned the key to start my car and drive back to their office, one lawyer handed me a personal check as he wept. Another one supplied the plants for the small community garden our kids grew at the school for the "grammas" in the neighborhood. We ran our program for two years before the building was finally sold to the community for its use.

By the way, there's no expiration date on this sense of mission and purpose. One older SWW from Oklahoma describes how she's still driven to change careers and finish an education that will allow her to accomplish goals, many of which will take more years to achieve:

My career goal is to teach parenting skills to families where there are deaf or hearing-impaired family members. For example, at age sixty-three, I am pursuing a master's degree to become a licensed professional counselor. This is one of the final steps on a path that started with parenting my own children, thirty-nine years ago. At age forty-eight, I went back to school to gain my credentials as a sign language interpreter and to acquire language and cultural skills to equip me to better understand the deaf/hearing-impaired experience and identity. So you see, I've been pursuing this goal for fifteen years without stopping.

SWWs are almost never content to coast—we feel the need to keep pedaling. We're constantly on the lookout for something that needs to be done: a wrong that needs to be righted, a circumstance that has to be changed, a system that must be improved. We want to stay in motion, learning and adjusting as we go. Boredom can be our greatest enemy.

We're Always Ready for a Challenge

We're energized by finding answers to problems no one else has been able to solve. In fact, we've been known to become offended if we aren't given a chance to help create a plan to deal with the current dilemma, especially if it turns into a full-blown crisis. Athena puts it like this: "I'm best when I can step into a chaotic situation, take charge, figure things out, and get things accomplished."

While others may be willing to take no for an answer, we're not daunted by the impossible or fearful of blazing new trails. When others turn around at the Road Closed sign, we think, *There has to be a way to get through there.*

If we're passionate about an issue, we don't just sit back and hope that eventually someone will say something. We step up. We speak out. And if the ones who need to hear it don't listen, we're determined to keep sending the message until they do.

Imagine that you were up against an overwhelming problem that desperately needed to be solved, but you couldn't see any apparent solution. What kind of friend would you ask for advice? Who would you want to pray for you? I'd head straight for an SWW who has a solid relationship with God, wouldn't you?

We Never Want to Give Up

One of an SWW's best traits is persistence. We don't give up; we don't quit. We push through hardships, knock down walls, and never say die. At its best, our will keeps us going and gives us the strength and determination to overcome even some of the most difficult obstacles.

Elizabeth offers a good example: "I forge ahead in spite of extreme or even ridiculous resistance, oppression, discrimination, resentment. If I'm sure God called me to it, I'm in until He moves me out or gives me permission to leave."

And Lisa insists her persistence is an asset: "I'm determined and relentless! I'm willing to politely badger people if needed."

WHEN GOOD STRONG WILL GOES BAD

There's no question that being an SWW can be a definite plus, but that same intensity and passion, if not consciously kept in check, can become a destructive force. We might call it the dark side of strong will. We all recognize it when it happens, and once it takes a wrong turn, it's tough to steer it back on course.

Sometimes in the middle of an argument or confrontation I have known full well what I should say or do next but instead watched myself go down in flames. If you're nodding as you read this, you know exactly what I mean. Once the negative response is triggered, it's difficult to stop firing the bullets.

One of my favorite descriptions of this occurrence comes from Loann's survey:

> I've often said that when my strong will takes a turn for the worse, it looks like this: I think of a cartoon where a bulldozer has just flattened all the characters. Then I look back and see the bodies and wonder how they got flattened . . . and then I realize that I'm the one who's been driving the bulldozer. *Oops!* Time to pick up the pieces.

We experience a constant struggle between dark and light when it comes to using our strong will—especially under stress or in the middle of a crisis. We know in our heads what needs to be done, and since we're wired for action, we can easily push into a situation without paying enough attention to who else is already there. We have inborn radar that detects injustice, so we may jump in without thoroughly verifying all the facts or checking the vital stats of others involved.

Without God's direction, our righteous indignation can quickly become just plain indignation as we jettison the righteous part. We can get so caught up in our outrage that even our best intentions alienate others and we end up hurting the very cause we support by overlooking the importance of how we deal with those who stand in our way. Debe's survey comment sums it up well: "I can devour people as I complete my tasks. I am misinterpreted as domineering, bossy, and mean. I can try and take over things that aren't in my control."

One SWW in Indiana wrote, "I'm firm. My strong will tends to surface when referencing matters of faith, child rearing, homeschooling, health, and nutrition. These are all things where I don't see any benefit in wavering. When I love deeply, how could I possibly be willing to do less than what I believe is best?"

Did you catch the red flag in that last sentence? *How could I possibly be willing to do less than what I believe is best.* No wonder we carry a lot of potential for creating tension and misunderstanding—especially when we insist on what *we* think is best.

Since we easily identified the top ten benefits of having a strong will, it's only fair that we admit to a few drawbacks. So here's a list of the top ten ways our strong will can go sideways.

What Happens When Our Strong Will Takes the Wrong Direction?

I . . .

- turn into a wall that can't be moved
- dig in my heels even when I'm wrong and try to make the other person appear as wrong as I am
- become controlling or manipulative
- become judgmental when others don't see things my way
- am usually slow to apologize
- can be obnoxious when competing, especially if I'm losing
- have no patience
- become overbearing and run over others when trying to get things done
- act or speak too quickly in an attempt to make things happen instead of trusting the Lord
- become bossy and irritable

Remember, these are not traits of a strong-willed woman—these are traits of a strong will that's gone *sideways*. There's a big difference. It's not that we *want* to make others feel bad—it's just that our pesky, take-charge nature often gets us in trouble. I like the way Kate puts it: "I become so bossy and irritable I can't even stand *myself*!"

Sally's dilemma sums up the way a lot of us feel:

> I often feel my "well, someone just needs to provide direction for this project to get it completed" attitude is outside what I believe people are comfortable with. I feel people think, *Wow, she is pushy!* rather than appreciate what I am able to accomplish. The lifestyle of a strong woman can be lonely. But is that my fault? Should I turn it down a notch? I know slowing down would help in developing relationships—I have a couple dear friends who are strong women, but we're all too busy making a difference to make time for lunch!

SO WHAT'S A STRONG-WILLED WOMAN TO DO?

Thousands of self-help and self-improvement books, which you'll probably never read, offer strategies for taking control of your life and making your strong will work to accomplish your goals. There's no shortage of advice for how you can demand your rights and protest unfair treatment, or for effective ways to conquer your enemies. That's not what this book is about.

We aren't talking about women who are just strong willed. We're talking about women with strength and purpose who, above all, desire to use their strong wills to bring honor and glory to God. Remember this: there is a stark contrast between an SWW *with* God and an SWW *without* God. If we're committed to living all out for Him, it will mean that sometimes what we do will be opposed to what the world insists is necessary for victory. Galatians 2:20 explains it this way: "My old self has been crucified with Christ. It is no longer I who live, but Christ lives in me. So I live in this earthly body by trusting in the Son of God, who loved me and gave himself for me" (NLT).

We're committed to living up to a higher standard, using our strength and potential in ways that will not harm, that will point others to the God who created us for His purposes. That means we don't use our strong will as an excuse for bad behavior or a justification for stubbornness or a reason for exerting control over others. Most of all, it means that we agree to allow God to work in us and to shape us to be in line with His will, and that takes a conscious act of *our* wills—to surrender to Him, to let Him take over.

Throughout this book, you'll find SWWs who admit we don't always get it right, even when we try with all our might. But we've also learned that when we commit our hearts and minds to God and when we're vigilant in how we use our strength and purpose, it really does make all the difference in the world.

WE'RE EVERYWHERE

Many years ago I was speaking to a group of youth workers in the Caribbean Republic of Trinidad and Tobago. I was the only Caucasian among them. They were a warm, receptive audience. I've always insisted that the learning-style concepts I teach transcend race, creed, color, religion, and politics—and this was certainly my chance to prove it. Other than leaving out a few purely American examples, I gave the same presentation I make in the United States. Would the message be relevant? Would I make sense to a culture and population so different from mine?

In the afternoon I shared with them about my strong-willed nature and how I had learned—sometimes the hard way—that it could only be an asset when I used it for God's purposes.

After the session was over, one woman quickly approached me. She was at least twenty years older than I was, and in physical appearance we couldn't have been more different. She was as short as I am tall, and her skin was as dark as mine is fair. She grinned as she hugged me and said, "You're just like me!" We talked for a few minutes and discovered that when it came to how we think and process information, we could practically be twins. Her strong will had gotten her into trouble when she was younger too, but once she dedicated her heart and will to God, she was delighted to find that He had made her that way on purpose, and her strength and determination were making a huge difference as she spread the gospel in Trinidad and beyond.

Over the past thirty years I've discovered SWWs serving God all over the world, each representing rich diversity, incredible talents, and amazing abilities. There are no geographical boundaries and no language or culture barriers for women of strength and purpose. They span the globe, surrounding the entire world with infinite possibilities and potential. It's a privilege to be counted among them, and it's truly humbling to think that God chooses to use us in such unique and wonderful ways.

LIVING **ALL OUT** FOR *God*

I s it even *possible* for a woman with a strong will to be a Christian?" The question came from Susan, a young, athletically built woman who approached me before I was going to give my SWW seminar. Before I could say anything, she continued. "I mean, I don't really go for that touchy-feely stuff—or anything else that seems emotional or fluffy. Is that what I'd have to do in order to be considered a *Christian* strong-willed woman?"

I sat with her in the back row of the room and listened as she told me about her background. The way she put it, she was an "off the charts" SWW. She'd grown up with Christian parents, but she'd taken a serious detour when she hit middle school. Her strong will had made her a natural leader among her peers, but when her parents objected to some of the kids she was hanging around with, she rebelled by getting new friends who were the type they wouldn't approve of at all.

"I was a wild child," she admitted. "But I've come back around and settled down a lot since college." She leaned forward and added, "I know I should make things right with God, but to tell you the truth, I don't want to give up everything that made me strong enough to walk away in the first place."

Even though Susan's background was different from mine, I understood what she was talking about. Every SWW has her own unique story about coming to Christ, but all of us struggle at some point with how to turn our stubborn, independent heart and disposition over to the only One who truly knows what to do with it.

My dad was an evangelical pastor for more than fifty years, and he was my strong-willed hero and role model from the moment I was born. He had grown up in what he terms "deep sin," but he and his strong will were gloriously saved when he was in the navy in World War II. He felt God call him to preach, and that's what he did—although he paid an unthinkable price to do it. His atheist father disowned him and cut him off from the rest of his family.

We lived in Las Vegas during my early and late teens, and I got a lot of what I call spiritual field trips. Dad's heart was full of love and compassion for the lost, and his ministry included some of the most destitute and wayward souls. I watched him live his message as consistently at home as he did from the pulpit. I understood from a young age that a life totally committed to Christ was uncompromising in its requirement of full surrender. I marveled at how someone so strong and confident as my dad could be so tender and obedient to God, and I saw how his commitment yielded amazing results.

While my story is different from my dad's and I never really rebelled against my parents, I certainly wasn't an angel growing up. I valued my close relationship with Dad too much to stray far, and I stayed close to what I knew was important to him. In the end, it wasn't the prospect of a future in heaven or avoiding eternal damnation that drew me to give my heart unconditionally to God (although both of those are certainly a bonus). It was the promise of a close, personal relationship with Jesus Christ—the kind my dad had with Him, and the kind I had with my dad.

For some SWWs, it takes a harder lesson for them to understand God's love and who they are in His kingdom. I love reading the story that SWW Liz Curtis Higgs tells of her faith journey. She was a self-described bad girl who, before her conversion, had pretty much tried all the wrong things, including drugs and alcohol. Liz says of her condition before giving her life completely to Christ: "I'm one of those people who had to fall all the way down to the bottom of the pit before I was forced to look up for help."[1] Liz is one of the most incredible SWWs I've ever known, and her ministry of speaking and writing continues to make a profound difference for God in the lives of countless women.

Whether you were more of a church girl or a reformed bad girl, if you're an SWW, you have wrestled, or will at some point, with three major concepts that are at the core of our Christian faith.

OUR STUMBLING BLOCKS TO FULLY SURRENDERING TO GOD

Repentance

Repentance is a word that has a negative connotation for many SWWs. Susan struggled with this because she had the impression that it was all part of the "touchy-feely" stuff she made a point of avoiding. Anyway, she wondered, was it possible for a person just to sin as much as she wanted and then, as long as she was willing to get all emotional and admit she had been wrong, God would forgive her again and again? That seemed like a weak approach to Susan, and she was suspicious that it wouldn't work in the long run.

But repentance means actively turning away from sin. It's

the way to God, and it comes only through accepting what Jesus Christ did for us on the cross. It's not primarily an emotional experience. It's the strong and deliberate surrender of our wills to Him.

Here's how Eugene Peterson describes repentance in his book *A Long Obedience in the Same Direction:*

> Repentance is not an emotion. It is not feeling sorry for your sins. It is a decision. It is deciding that you have been wrong in supposing that you could manage your own life and be your own god; it is deciding that you were wrong in thinking that you had, or could get, the strength, education and training to make it on your own. . . . And it is deciding that God in Jesus Christ is telling you the truth. . . . Repentance is a decision to follow Jesus Christ and become his pilgrim in the path of peace.[2]

C. S. Lewis explained that repentance "is not something God demands of you before He will take you back and which He could let you off if He chose: it is simply a description of what going back to Him is like."[3] It is basically a U-turn. Instead of going away from God, or ignoring Him, you turn around, go to Him, and choose to give Him His rightful place in your life. Repentance, therefore, has more to do with your will than it has to do with your feelings.

There's nothing weak about that! Repentance means taking strong, decisive action, and SWWs can respect that. It's also clear that no one can make us repent. It's strictly our decision, and the timing is our call. Christ doesn't knock down the door of our hearts and insist we let Him in. He respects the strong will He designed in us too much to do that. Instead He waits patiently for us to grant Him entry. He says, "Here I am! I stand at the door and knock. If anyone hears my voice and opens the door, I will come in and eat with that person, and they with me" (Revelation 3:20, NIV).

Once you've overcome this stumbling block and chosen to confess and seek forgiveness, you're faced with the next act of will—and it may seem even harder than repentance.

Submission

The thought of simply handing over control to someone else and meekly following the leader is not appealing to SWWs—so it's a good thing that's not what submission to God means. True submission is the voluntary surrender of control to our Creator and Designer, who knows and loves us unconditionally and who truly wants what is best for us. We accept this submission by *choice*. Far from being an admission of defeat, our surrender to Jesus represents a victory over our own selfish will and desires.

Submission isn't a passive, soft, quiet act. One of my favorite verses in the King James Version of the Bible is 2 Corinthians 10:5: "Casting down imaginations, and every high thing that exalteth itself against the knowledge of God, and bringing into captivity every thought to the obedience of Christ." As an SWW, I like the visual picture of taking swift and decisive action to bring into captivity any thought or activity that doesn't honor God. I want to *track* it down, *take* it captive, and *turn* it over to God.

The term *submission* takes on a whole new meaning when you realize that the One you are surrendering to will never take advantage of your trust. He will forever be your one true foundation, and you can confidently build your life on Him.

Most SWWs agree that submission to God represents the highest level of victory over our own self-centeredness—but it does take daily discipline to stay firmly and unshakably surrendered to Christ. All of us humanly struggle with the whole idea of *surrender,* and if we're honest, most of us fight almost daily battles to resist jumping back in and directing our own lives when it seems as if God might not be getting it right. For SWWs, it may sometimes feel like torture. But it's essential to our purpose that we work on this aspect of our spiritual lives.

Rick Warren, pastor and author of *The Purpose Driven Life,* shows us what submission at work really looks like: "You know you're surrendered to God when you rely on God to work things out instead of trying to manipulate others, force your agenda, and control the situation. You let go and let God work. You don't have to always be 'in charge.' . . . Instead of trying harder, you trust more."[4]

Submission is at the core of our ability to use our strong will to make a positive difference in our lives, our relationships, our work, and our world. It's that important and that powerful.

But if that doesn't sound strong enough yet, wait until you hear the *next* stumbling block.

Obedience

The idea of obedience may be the most misunderstood when it comes to how an SWW perceives a personal relationship with Jesus Christ. The word *obey* can bring to mind an image of a child waiting for an authoritarian parent to tell her what to do—definitely not appealing to SWWs.

But obedience—as referred to by Christ—always carries with it a choice. Just as God doesn't force us to repent or submit, He doesn't *make* us obey Him. Of course, we shouldn't be surprised if there are consequences when we disobey.

As difficult as it may feel for us to practice obedience, the good news is that choosing to obey, using our strength to listen to and follow the voice of God, can be the most exhilarating and rewarding thing we'll ever do. After all, we're naturally drawn to challenges, and we're not daunted by the seemingly impossible task of offering obedience to the God of the whole universe.

Of course, not *all* obedience will entail new and grand adventures. Once we SWWs fully commit to obeying God, we can sometimes be disappointed if He *doesn't* give us big tasks to do—after all, we have a strong will that can accomplish great things!

Alison Dellenbaugh, in a blog for *Christianity Today,* recounts her frustration that God wasn't asking her to do more—why wasn't He using her to minister in bigger ways?

"Here I am. Send me!" we say with Isaiah. "Anything! Anywhere!" We're ready to lay down our lives, take up our crosses, and follow Jesus into even rough waters. Go to Africa? Start an orphan care ministry? Plant a church in the inner city? No matter how big, Lord, we'll do it!

But what if God asks us to do something *small*? That can be the hardest calling of all, especially for those of us who feel passionate about following him with abandon and making a difference in the world.[5]

I don't know about you, but I'm often guilty of overlooking the importance of a million small ways to obey because I'm scanning the horizon for the next big challenge. But Jesus reminds us in Luke 16:10, "Whoever can be trusted with very little can also be trusted with much" (NIV). Obedience—both in big ways and small ones—matters if we want to live a life of strength and purpose.

What's It Like to Live All Out for God?

Repentance requires a firm decision to turn our lives around; *submission* takes daily discipline to stay firmly and unshakably surrendered to Christ; *obedience* demands a vigorous and energetic commitment to strike out into the unknown and be willing to conquer the impossible. That sounds like Christianity was tailor-made for those of us with strong wills.

Many years ago, in the role of an educational consultant, I was working with a police sergeant on some training materials for a local police department. When we got to the section titled "Officer Safety," the sergeant paused, looked up at me, and said, "You know, technically, there's no such thing as 'officer safety.' It's not a safe profession."

Living all out for God certainly doesn't mean we'll have a *safe* life. It's not *supposed* to be safe—*or* particularly easy. That doesn't mean it always has to be full of turmoil and trials; it just means we want so much of God that we're willing to do whatever He asks us to do. It also means we have a rock-solid faith and a deep, abiding joy that doesn't depend on our circumstances.

One of the biggest reasons SWWs are such excellent candidates for God's special ops team is that we're willing to keep going when others give up. He can count on us to step up and take assignments that call for more courage, extra faith, and unrelenting effort. Imagine how frustrated the Enemy must be when he realizes who God has put him up against in the battle!

How do we get those assignments? Although God engages us in a variety of ways to recognize His voice, one of my favorites is what I refer to as a Holy Spirit Nudge, or HSN. It can happen to anyone, but SWWs often have the least hesitation to act on it. It's when you get an inexplicable sense that you should do something—make a phone call, start a conversation with a stranger, visit a specific place at a particular time. Perhaps someone's name comes to mind, or on a whim, you desire to go to a different restaurant than usual, or you feel as though you should write someone a letter, or you just have this irresistible urge to do something completely out of character for you. It's often God sending an intuitive signal, an HSN, that someone has a need that you can meet, a connection that could be important later, a solution to a problem you didn't even know you had.

If you're walking close to God, staying in tune with Him through prayer, and asking for His guidance and direction, you'll get a surprising amount of HSNs—all you need is the confidence to follow them. And when you do, what's your reward? You get to be the answer to someone's prayer. Oswald Chambers explains it like this:

> Our lives, my life, is the answer to someone's prayer, prayed perhaps centuries ago. . . . I have the unspeakable knowledge that my life is the answer to prayers, and that God is blessing me and making me a blessing entirely of His sovereign grace and nothing to do with my merits, saving as I am bold enough to trust His leading and not the dictates of my own wisdom and common sense.[6]

That's a responsibility not everyone is willing to shoulder. What if God has designed you to answer prayers that no one else could answer? What if your strong will is exactly what He wants to use to accomplish His purposes? What if, by living close to Him, you could be the link that helps rescue the lost, encourage the weary, and lift even the most defeated? It may not always be a big deal—you may not even get earthly credit or recognition—but God sees, and He has a customized plan designed with you in mind. Sometimes it just takes an SWW to get it done.

PROFILES IN
Perseverance

LILY HO SIPE

You've never met a hairstylist like Lily Ho Sipe. Measuring less than five feet tall, this dynamic, petite, strong-willed woman is a bundle of continuous motion and high energy. She owns the building that houses her hairstyling business. Her home sits high atop a huge hill above Puyallup, Washington. She and her husband built it with large Bible studies and prayer groups in mind. Within the first few sentences of a conversation, Lily introduces the topic of Jesus or prayer. She asks every client the same question: "How can I pray for you today?" This is not a casual question; she knows God answers prayer. She's living proof that He does the impossible.

Lily was born in Taiwan as a member of the fourth generation of a faithful Christian family, even though she would not truly embrace Christ as her personal Savior until she was an adult. Her father died when she was one year old. The family was so poor that Lily's mom moved to Taipei to work, leaving Lily and her older brother with their grandparents, who were very poor, to raise them. Although her mom promised to visit once a year, Lily doesn't remember seeing her at all until her seventh birthday. After that brief visit, she did not see her mother again until Lily turned twenty years of age. Her mom came not only to visit but also to make her daughter an irresistible offer.

She revealed that she had married an American man several years earlier and now they were living in the States. She looked closely at Lily and offered to sponsor her so she could move to the United States too. All her young life Lily had dreamed of being rich and successful, and she eagerly accepted her mother's offer. She couldn't believe she was suddenly getting such a wonderful opportunity!

In August 1978 at age twenty, Lily moved to Everett, Washington. She knew she wanted to do something extraordinary. She wanted the American dream—money, position, success. There was, however, one major problem. She didn't speak a word of English. Her strong will kicked in, and she doggedly pursued any job where she could learn English while earning a little money.

Lily realized right away that she needed to be trained in a skill if she wanted to get anywhere, so she immediately looked for opportunities. She learned that the city of Everett was offering a scholarship for seven people to attend beauty school for a year to become certified hairdressers. It wasn't what she originally had in mind, but she knew she could easily do that, and it would no doubt be her ticket to bigger things.

Lily applied for the scholarship and took the required test. Soon she learned that she had passed the test with flying colors—but, unfortunately, she was number eight on the list of seven. Lily was not crushed with disappointment, though, because she was certain this was only a temporary setback. God would surely help her find a way.

She decided to pray every day that someone would drop out of the program and give her a place.

She went back every day at first, but the city officials kept saying, "There's no chance. Sorry." Rather than give up, she called at least twice a week. Her strong will made her very determined.

After four or five weeks, they called her. "This is really strange," said the city employee. "Usually no one gives up a position in the program, but one person actually has done that. Since you're the only one who has kept calling us, we're going to give that position to you."

Lily breezed through the training, perfected her English, married Rob, a handsome American, and began to climb the ladder of success she had always dreamed about. But then another barrier blocked her goals.

After Lily and Rob got married, they learned they could never have a baby. Lily was frustrated. "I was sure that if you just worked hard, you could get whatever you want," she said. "But there's a certain point when you begin to realize that no matter how hard you work, it's up to God if you get what you want." But her strong-willed nature wasn't ready to just give up and let God do His work without her help. After trying all kinds of fertility methods and treatments, Lily decided she would negotiate with the Creator of the universe—after all, He could do anything, right?

"If You bless me with a baby," Lily told God, "I will give an offering to the church. They need a copy machine, so I'll give it to them." Without waiting for an answer, she bought the copy machine and confidently started the next fertility procedure. But it failed.

Lily had a stern talk with God. *God, You didn't keep your end of the bargain!* Then she thought, *Maybe I didn't give enough.* She discovered that the church couldn't afford the roof they needed since it was going to cost thousands of dollars. She said, *Okay, God. I'll buy the roof for them if You'll just let me have a baby.*

They had tried for three years to conceive, but this time when her doctor called, he said, "Lily, we've tried everything humanly possible. There's nothing more we can do."

Lily wept and prayed. "I realized no matter how hard I tried to get things done using my own strong will, it was not enough." Finally, she prayed, "Okay, God. If You want me to serve You and not have children, I'm willing to surrender to You. I've done my best." Lily admits it had taken almost forty years of living a Christian life before she truly let God have everything her heart, her soul, and finally her strong will.

She told everyone who had been praying for her and supporting her efforts that she was done trying—no more struggling to have a baby.

A few months later, Lily got a call from someone who had a friend who was placing a baby up for adoption. Would she and her husband be interested? Lily was stunned. Was this God's answer to her prayers? She hadn't even considered it would happen this way. She was humbled, realizing it was only *after* she was truly willing to surrender her strong will completely and let God do what *He* had in mind that the impossible happened. With a new joy in her heart, Lily opened her arms to her beautiful daughter, Hannah.

But God wasn't finished surprising her yet. Six years later, Lily's doctor told her "something really bad" was going on in her body, and she would need to have a hysterectomy. As they tried to schedule the operation, things kept coming up to delay it. It was almost two months before they were able to book the procedure. Two weeks before her surgery, Lily got an unexpected call from her grandmother in Taiwan.

"We keep praying for you to have a baby," her grandmother told her. Lily didn't have the heart to tell her she was going to have a hysterectomy in a couple weeks, providing a permanent answer to that prayer. After she hung up, she thought, *Hmm. I haven't had my monthly period for a while. I'd better call the doctor and make sure everything's all right.* She went in for some tests, and later that afternoon the nurse called back to tell her she was *pregnant.* Lily couldn't believe it! She says that as soon as she hung up, God clearly spoke to her: *You're going to have a son, and you are to name him Isaac Luke.*

Lily's pregnancy had almost every kind of complication and problem possible. She was forty-one, and the doctor warned her that at her age there was a high risk of genetic abnormalities and hinted that she might not want to carry the pregnancy to term. But Lily had lots of practice using her strong will to trust God. She told the doctor, "It doesn't matter. God is giving me this baby, and when God gives you a special gift, you don't let the devil take it away."

A few months later, Isaac Luke Sipe was born completely healthy, and Lily was more convinced than ever that God is in control. "I have learned not to depend upon my own power. God's power is the only thing that really works."

WHAT'S **WRONG** WITH *Being* SELF-SUFFICIENT?

I t was the Easter season, and the pastor asked for volunteers from the congregation to write in big black letters a sin they had been delivered from, thanks to the sacrifice of Christ on the cross. At least two dozen people walked up, drew their signs, and held them up all across the platform. Most of the sins were familiar—drugs, alcohol, infidelity, dishonesty. But one woman's sign stood out, at least to any other SWW watching. The sign read "Self-Sufficiency."

Wait. How is that a sin? Isn't being self-sufficient a *good* thing? After all, aren't we taught to think for ourselves, to be independent and self-reliant?

Ann, one of my SWW friends, is a former FBI agent who left her career to be a full-time mom of two beautiful young daughters. Since her husband travels extensively for business, she uses her strong will, in part, to keep her household running smoothly. She's one of the most independent and efficient women I know. Because she's a woman of faith, many people admire her and she's a strong influence in her local church. In addition, she has used her skill and talent to stay involved with the community—creating fantastic outdoor displays for every holiday, taking volunteer classroom duty, organizing community events. She's truly awe inspiring. But last year Ann suddenly developed a serious type of cancer that requires very aggressive treatment.

She started a blog to describe how she was undaunted and how she still juggled all her responsibilities at home, even though it was more challenging. Her friends and family gathered around her, offering to help, but she insisted she could handle everything on her own. Her husband still traveled, her kids still did well in school, and the house still looked pretty good. But a few months later, Ann hit a wall. Her body simply refused to be as determined as her heart and mind, and she ended up spending several days in the hospital.

As much as Ann hated to admit it, she couldn't keep doing everything herself. Her faithful friends rallied and organized a food brigade, her family stepped up to take over school duties, her husband temporarily curtailed his travel schedule to spend more time at her side. Ann's Facebook page was filled with posts from many of these helpers—they were ecstatic that she let them be there for her. Ann was surprised at how the revelation of her need was drawing everyone in her sphere of influence closer, not only to her but also to one another, and she said she'd never felt more loved and blessed by God.

We really do need each other, whether or not we like to admit it. Sometimes SWWs don't want to ask people for help because we don't want to bother them—or, secretly, we might think we could just do it better ourselves. But often the real reason is deeper than that. We don't have any problem motivating people to join us in helping *others,* but it feels weak and almost shameful to ask or allow someone to help us. Our independent nature tends to consider it a measure of our character to press on without asking for assistance.

Amy understands this struggle. On her survey, she wrote, "I'm a doer and a fixer and a ridiculous multitasker. I help everyone but don't leave room for receiving help. If I'm not careful, I take control and forget to let God lead."

Here we are, thinking that we're the ones in charge and no one has to help us, and yet what we may forget is that our refusal of assistance can rob someone else of the blessing and affirmation that comes from being *able* to contribute. It turns out that accepting help isn't weak; it actually takes more strength and courage to admit we need help than to forge ahead without it. In fact, the most important benefit when we say yes to a friend or family member who offers a helping hand is that we actually strengthen that relationship by letting that person perform a labor of love for us.

HOW MUCH HELP DOES GOD WANT FROM ME?

Just as we struggle with doing it all and refusing to allow others to help, sometimes we think that God wants us to do it all when we're serving Him too. As SWWs, we are capable of solving difficult problems, working through complicated issues, tackling insurmountable obstacles. But God doesn't want our self-sufficiency. He wants our obedience. It *is* a balancing act. After all, we want to roll up our sleeves and do our part, but we don't want to get ahead of God—and we don't want to take a road that leads away from doing His will. So how do we know when we're following God's plan as opposed to taking off under our own power?

I was wrestling with this problem a few years ago, so I decided to call my SWW friend Jan Silvious, who is a fellow speaker and author.

"Jan," I said, "I've always promised God I wouldn't knock down a door He has firmly closed. But as long as that door is still even a *little* ajar, I'm going to keep pushing on it."

She laughed and agreed.

I continued. "How do you determine the difference between a door that God has closed and one that just presents another obstacle to be overcome?"

I'll never forget her answer, because it has continued to help me years later. "Well, Cynthia," she replied with her sweet Tennessee accent, "I've always just figured that as long as I have a 'holy want-to,' the door's still open. When I lose that holy want-to, God has closed it."

Obviously a person has to walk close to God in order to recognize that holy want-to. But there's no doubt that God can do extraordinary things through SWWs who aren't afraid to push on a few doors.

Too often our problem is that, in our self-sufficient state, we act as though God needs a little nudge or advice from us—as though the world would work better if He at least had a suggestion box. He doesn't, although sometimes I wish He did! As an SWW, I'm never at a loss for suggestions on how things should be done.

Of course, it doesn't matter how *good* my ideas are—if they're not *God's* ideas, they will ultimately fail. We can have the best of intentions, the purest of motives, and still fall short in God's eyes if we insist on doing everything in our own strength. Brandi admits this about her own life: "I'm persistent and determined to accomplish my goals, but I'm learning that these traits work in my favor when I follow God, and they fall apart when I get outside His plan and try to lead. Hopefully I've made the last trip around that mountain."

BUT HOW IS SELF-SUFFICIENCY A SIN?

Do you ever catch yourself worrying about whether God is doing the right thing in a particular circumstance? Could He have misunderstood the situation? Does He realize how important it is? Perhaps this sounds ridiculous to most people, but SWWs have asked these questions. I can get so used to handling everything and guiding outcomes and circumstances that I can actually find myself questioning the Creator of the universe. That's when I realize how my self-sufficiency can become a sin. In *My Utmost for His Highest,* Oswald Chambers puts the idea this way:

> Fretting springs from a determination to get our own way. Our Lord never worried and He was never anxious, because He was not "out" to realize His own ideas; He was "out" to realize God's ideas. Fretting is wicked if you

are a child of God. . . . All our fret and worry is caused by calculating without God.[1]

SWWs value being able to control our lives, and we take pride in the fact that we can usually help others take control of theirs. Like good trial attorneys, we don't ask any questions if we don't already know the answers. But that approach just doesn't work with God. Let's face it—the woman who is totally self-sufficient makes no room for God to surprise her, to demonstrate His power, His love, or His gifts.

To combat the sin of self-sufficiency, we need a special kind of faith. It's what I call Starbucks Rest Room Faith. Almost every Starbucks store has a sensor that controls the light in the rest room. You can't just flip a switch, and you can't make it go on by just waving your arm inside the door. You have to put your whole body into that dark room and trust that the light will come on as you enter. Faith in God is a lot like that. He doesn't offer a safety net, He doesn't let us hedge our bets, and He doesn't give any guaranteed results ahead of time. We have to be all in before the light comes on.

There was a pivotal time early in my career when I learned this for myself. I had given up a steady income as a teacher to start my own business as a speaker and author. My mother was my only employee, but she had shifted her duties to provide day care for my twin sons. As the demand for my books and seminars increased, it became obvious that I needed to hire another employee. There wasn't enough money to pay another salary, but we needed a second employee if the business was going to keep growing. Since my husband had suffered a major illness and wasn't yet ready to work full time, we had almost no financial reserves.

I admit I worried about it a lot, but every time I prayed about the situation, I felt in my heart that I was supposed to stick with the business and not go back to teaching full time. But where would the money come from?

One Sunday as I sat in the pew and prayed again for guidance, our pastor shared a compelling story. He said when he was a young preacher, his church grew like crazy. He and the church board agreed they needed to hire an associate pastor. They prayed about it, voted on it, and agreed to trust God to bring in the extra offerings to hire the new associate. Weeks passed, but they received no additional offerings. My pastor was discouraged and overburdened with work, so he sought out his mentor, a retired preacher and evangelist.

"I don't understand," said my pastor. "In Philippians 4:19, Paul offers the promise that God shall supply all our needs. We have a desperate need. We've prayed about it and we've claimed the promise, but God hasn't provided the income."

The older clergyman nodded sympathetically, then asked

what seemed like a ridiculous question. "Have you hired the associate?"

The young pastor was surprised. "No, of course not—we can't afford it."

The older gentleman replied gently, "Then you don't have a need. If you've prayed through on this and you believe God wants you to do it, hire the associate. Then you'll have a need, and God can supply it."

As I sat listening to that story, I knew what I had to do: I was supposed to step out in faith and hire that new employee so the business could move forward. I did exactly that. Now, more than twenty-five years later, I can tell you that having the faith to walk into that dark room has yielded more wonderful blessings than I could have ever imagined.

Paul wrote in 1 Corinthians 13:12 that growing in our faith requires us to accept that we cannot see the whole picture. God knows the past, the present, and the future: "We don't yet see things clearly. We're squinting in a fog, peering through a mist. But it won't be long before the weather clears and the sun shines bright! We'll see it all then, see it all as clearly as God sees us, knowing him directly just as he knows us!"

Having the faith to trust God—to rely on Him—in the mist and fog of life's challenges is a critical part of our Christian walk. We'll never fully experience God's faithfulness if we don't allow Him the opportunity to show us how to do that.

Years ago we sang a little chorus in church called "It's Jesus and Me." It went like this: "It is Jesus and me for each tomorrow; for every heartache and every sorrow . . . " I used to feel pretty good, thinking about how I was taking Jesus with me wherever I went. Yep, we were constant companions, Jesus and me. Then a few years ago our pastor reminded us that it doesn't work that way. Jesus says "Follow Me," not the other way around. Oh. Wow. That's a lot harder to do. That's putting aside my self-sufficiency and working in faith to trust His direction and leading.

It may take all we've got to keep from giving God the good advice that just bubbles up in us—but that's when we need to use our strong will to pick up the Bible or get on our knees . . . and follow Him.

WE'RE NOT DESIGNED TO GO IT ALONE

One of the most amazing and wonderful benefits of being an SWW totally committed to God is that we no longer have the pressure of being in charge of everything. Now, to many people, that sounds pretty good—but for the SWW it's a double-edged sword. On the one hand, we have incredible strength and power to do good by making reliance on God and His Word our number one priority. On the other hand, it means allowing our wills to be transformed to *His* will—even if there are times when we're sure we have a better idea of how to get things done.

It means acknowledging that at some point we will face insurmountable obstacles and our strong will alone will not be able to sustain us. Everyone hits a wall eventually—just ask my friend, Ann, who struggled with cancer. The question is, will it drive us from God or draw us closer to Him?

First Corinthians 10:12–13 says: "Don't be so naive and self-confident. You're not exempt. You could fall flat on your face as easily as anyone else. Forget about self-confidence; it's useless. Cultivate God-confidence. No test or temptation that comes your way is beyond the course of what others have had to face. All you need to remember is that God will never let you down; he'll never let you be pushed past your limit; he'll always be there to help you come through it."

I don't know about you, but falling flat on my face has never been on my to-do list. In fact, even if it happens, it's the last thing I would have *asked* God to let happen to me—and I sure don't want to expose my failures to anyone else. But I realize that if I simply make it a matter of pride, I'm not going to learn what God may be trying to teach me. If I trust Him, I believe my pain can have a purpose, and that in the greater scheme of His plan, it will be woven into the fabric of His will.

Jean Daly, a fellow SWW and wife of Focus on the Family's president, Jim Daly, tells a compelling story of the journey that brought this concept home to her:

When I was thirty-one, my thirty-three-year-old brother, whom I adored, committed suicide. My world came crashing down. Depression took me deep into its grip, and the blackness and hopelessness were crushing. I was absolutely broken. I was convinced that I couldn't survive the pain—I didn't want to endure it. Since I believed that God would not give me more than I could handle, and since I felt for sure that my brother's death was definitely more than I could handle, I was convinced God was going to somehow humanely end my life and whisk me to heaven. That probably sounds bizarre, but that is how much pain I was in.

But it didn't happen. I had to keep on living. In the bottomless pit of my despair I recognized that I was desperately trying to survive this loss in my own strength—and it was never going to be enough. I could not do this on my own. I knew I needed outside help. That's when I finally began going to a Christian counselor.

Counseling was a positive experience, but it was really difficult. It forced me to explore a number of tough issues. I had to address areas where I hadn't fully surrendered to God. The benefit from this life-altering counseling spread to my marriage and my entire perspective. I'm able to experience joy, peace, and contentment. I use my strength and determination to consciously surrender to Christ on a daily basis. It drives me to spend time in the Scriptures, which constantly remind me of the real truth of how much He loves me and how much I need Him.

My loss gave me a new depth of feeling and compassion for people in pain and has allowed me to talk to them about depression and encourage them to find help and hope. My relationship with the Lord has been deepened. While counseling and, when appropriate, medication may be helpful tools, they are not enough. True contentment and peace can come only from a totally committed relationship with Christ.

No SWW would ask for this kind of test of our resolve to fully trust God—but when the unthinkable happens, it's the strength of our commitment that keeps us firmly in His grasp. We never have to face the world alone.

BROKENNESS, ANYONE?

Several years ago we sang a worship song in church, "Take My Life (Holiness)." It had one verse I always skipped. I would listen to the people beside me sing, "Brokenness, brokenness is what I long for; brokenness is what I need . . ." I stood there and thought, *I'm not singing that! Who would ask for brokenness? Forget it!* Little did I know I was about to experience the very thing we sang about: a brokenness that would test the strength of my complete surrender to Christ.

Remember the woman in the beginning of this chapter who stood on the platform and held that sign that indicated self-sufficiency was the sin she'd been delivered from? That woman was me. After seventeen years of marriage, I made some jarring discoveries that had to do with betrayal and infidelity on the part of my husband. Despite intense counseling and intervention, we ended up going through a prolonged and painful divorce—an unimaginable outcome for this church girl who never saw it coming. How could this happen? What had I done? Why couldn't we work this out?

Suddenly I was facing a life-changing crisis that shook the foundation of my safe and familiar relationship with God to the core. The earthquake in my soul shattered every comfortable, well-known harbor I'd known and pushed me out to sea. I couldn't do anything but hold on to God for dear life. I was a strong-willed, independent, self-sufficient, successful woman who suddenly had lost control over my circumstances—and I was faced with truly God-sized needs. My professional reputation, my financial well-being, my ability to provide safety and security for my family—everything was at risk. During that dark season, all I had ever been taught to believe was stripped down to two simple words that I could almost hear God utter over and over: *Trust Me.*

The story is too long to tell here, but I can say that I had always figured I could handle pretty much anything that came my way. It took a crisis of huge proportions for me to understand the depth of His love for me and the unfathomable extent of His faithfulness. I had to get to the place where I was literally on my face before God, confessing I could not do it without Him. It was at this point of surrender that He rescued me.

I like to picture God as our perfect orchestra conductor. No matter how far off we get from the original score, God never misses a beat. He takes our mistakes, our failures, and our disappointments, and He blends them in as we go. And no matter what happens, when we're part of that orchestra, the music ends up sounding beautiful. That's what happens when we let go of our self-sufficiency to trust that He, our Conductor, really does know best.

JANINE TARTAGLIA METCALF

Janine Metcalf was a successful, strong-willed television reporter who was represented by one of the most sought-after agents in the prestigious William Morris Agency. Her greatest goal was to make it to New York and work for a network there. She got a job at KNBC in Los Angeles, which was wholly owned and operated by NBC, not just an affiliate. The next step was New York. She was on her way!

So how did an ambitious woman end up as a full-time pastor in a relatively small church in eastern Washington State? And why does she love it so much that she wouldn't trade places with anyone for anything in the world?

Janine was raised Roman Catholic. She grins when she remembers how this influenced her childhood. "When I was a child, I thought I was called to be a priest—I loved the sacrament, the Lord's Supper. I'd invite my friends over and tie two dish towels together around my neck for vestments. I'd serve communion—grape Kool-Aid and Necco wafers—and then I'd talk to my friends about Jesus."

As an adult, Janine went occasionally to church,

but when she became a television reporter, she became distracted from her faith. Television journalism is an all-consuming career, and soon it took over her entire life. Her name was on the big doors at KNBC, which opened to the news set where she anchored the weekend news.

Once as she was wandering around the studios, she came to one studio that was truly famous: *The Tonight Show*. She walked around Johnny Carson's set, sitting in his empty chair and pulling out the pencils he would toss as he talked to Ed McMahon. As she sat in that famous seat, she thought, *Here I am— I've made it to the network. Life is good . . . so why do I feel so absolutely empty?* She had college awards, local Emmy awards, and everything that most people would envy. But something was dreadfully wrong.

Then a life-changing event happened. It was November 1979, and the Iranian hostage crisis was headline news. Janine was assigned to shadow Earl and Hazel Lee, the parents of Gary Lee, one of the hostages. Earl was the beloved pastor of a large Nazarene church in Pasadena. Janine met with Earl and Hazel two or three times a week during the 444 days the hostages were held in Iran. During those visits she was impressed by how the Lees handled the stress and uncertainty of not knowing whether their son was dead or alive. "Earl Lee just walked Christ before me—and it made Jesus inviting, intriguing," she said. "I was in awe because Earl and Hazel Lee had something I knew I didn't have."

More than a year later, it looked as though the crisis was coming to an end. The Sunday morning a few days before the anticipated release of the hostages, a group of reporters decided to go to Earl Lee's church. Janine and her crew knew something was about to happen, and if the news broke during the service, they wanted to be there to capture the Lees' reaction, as well as the response of their parishioners who had prayed for the release. It would be a great story.

She brought her camera crew and joined the others who were setting up in the balcony. She knew that Earl Lee had been praying for her, as he told her that every time he invited her to church during those ten months. But Janine had always resisted. On this day, though, as she sat in that sanctuary, she unexpectedly realized she had already been captured by an entirely different story and the channel of her heart was tuned into something that was already going on in her spirit.

Everyone in the sanctuary wondered what Pastor Lee would say on such a momentous occasion. They knew things could go either way with the return of the hostages: they could walk off a plane and be just fine, or they could return dead. And it could all happen at any moment. The congregation watched Earl Lee step to the pulpit and open his Bible. He read from Isaiah 43:1–3 (NKJV):

> Fear not, for I have redeemed you; I have called you by your name; You are Mine. When you pass through the waters, I will be with you; and through the rivers, they shall not overflow you. When you walk through the fire, you shall not be burned, nor shall the flame scorch you. For I am the LORD your God, the Holy One of Israel, your Savior.

Janine's eyes light up as she recalls what happened next:

> Oh my goodness—the Lord spoke directly to me. His Spirit suddenly flooded me. My life had been in great turmoil for several weeks. There had been a shake-up in the newsroom: a change of news directors. Everything was unstable. I was uncertain and hurting and longing for peace. Although Pastor Lee did

not give a formal invitation to accept Jesus or ask anyone to stand if they were interested in making a commitment of some kind, I stood to my feet. I was overwhelmed with the sense of God's presence and His love for me, and if there had been a place to kneel, I would have dropped to my knees. I didn't know exactly what I was supposed to do, so I silently offered my simple confession to Him: *Oh God, I'm so sorry!*

She realized she had addressed everything in her life except her soul. Now something was going on so deep inside her that nothing else mattered. Her crew and the other reporters gave her strange looks, perhaps as though they wondered if she were trying to scout out a better camera angle.

Her cameraman whispered, "Janine! What are you doing?"

But she just kept standing. She didn't care what anyone else thought. She was no longer a reporter doing her job; she was a prodigal coming home to the arms of her Savior and heavenly Father. She was a strong-willed woman bending her knee to her Lord.

Previously, Earl had told her that if she would come to church, he would play his trumpet. Standing in that balcony, Janine saw him motion to his assistant to get something from his office, and when it was time for the huge choir to sing their special song, Pastor Earl Lee picked up his trumpet and joined in the chorus of "Glory, Glory Hallelujah!"

She said, "I was swept away from the world of journalism and into the arms of Jesus."

Later, when all the reporters were meeting in the parsonage with the Lee family, Earl quietly walked by Janine and inconspicuously dropped a packet of information into her lap about being a new believer. He let God work in His own time. He knew she would ask questions when she was ready.

The hostages were to be released a few days later. The State Department had given the press indications of their release, but nothing was certain. The situation was extremely unstable. No one knew if any of the hostages were alive.

Earl and Hazel opened their home to about twenty TV, radio, and newspaper reporters, and the people from Pasadena First Church fed all of them. Janine noticed that the church members were so kind that the normal atmosphere of fierce competition among the press gave way to a sense of camaraderie. There was a spirit of hopefulness in that house.

The hostages were released—and it was "go" time for Janine and the other reporters.

"We still didn't know if Gary was alive and free," she said. "We all gathered around the television, watching live as the hostages got off a plane that had just landed in Algiers." Hazel saw her son, Gary, first. "She almost screamed with joy. He had long hair and a long beard. She exclaimed, 'Oh! He looks like Jesus!' That room stuffed with reporters was filled with joy and peace."

Janine remained in television news less than a year after she became a Christian. Feeling strongly that she had to get out of the television news business, she left behind her dreams of a network career and stepped out—into nothing.

Janine enrolled at Fuller Theological Seminary in California and then traveled for a few years as an evangelist before joining the staff at Earl Lee's church. Later, she served as a full-time senior pastor in El Cajon, California, and then moved to Richland, Washington, where she became the pastor of the First Church of the Nazarene. Janine used her strong will to follow God into dreams that were so much better than the ones she originally thought she wanted. She is grateful she made that choice.

JUST BECAUSE **YOU** CAN
DOESN'T MEAN
You SHOULD

I f it's true the traits that make you most successful as an adult
got you in the most trouble when you were younger, you won't
be surprised by how many SWWs have large doses of both success *and* trouble!

One of the things that got me in the most trouble growing
up is what I like to call my gift of sarcasm. When you're younger,
they don't call it a gift. There are many other names for it—
smart mouth, smart aleck, back talker—but *gift* isn't one of

them. And yet, when I've used it appropriately, it's been a real plus in tense situations, especially as a teacher and a parent. It can inject just the right amount of humor when a student claims she's never taking another test and I reply, "Nice try," and smile. Or when my strong-willed son suggests he needs a more comfortable place to study and I ask him if he wants fries with that—and give him a grin.

Sarcasm was especially helpful during my six years as a police officer when I was determined not to use profanity. There's something about a calm, sarcastic reply to a suspect who's trying to impress you with his street vocabulary that just irritates him more than anything. Okay, okay, so I might have gotten in trouble a couple of times for "too smart a mouth" as an adult too. But for the most part, my gift of sarcasm helped me stick to my resolution not to swear to make my point.

Used with the right intention and in the right way, sarcasm can work well, but there is a drawback, of course. When SWWs use sarcasm inappropriately, we can slide sideways and end up tearing a path of destruction where we meant to just get in a small dig. We can be good with a quick comeback, a witty reply, a clever tease. But if things suddenly turn confrontational, it's hard not to take the bait and decimate our adversary.

There's a saying: "Those who anger you, control you." Every SWW knows we're gifted with a certain kind of resourcefulness that gives us an advantage when it comes to getting our way.

Our strong-willed natures are wired to take action, do what needs to be done, fight to the finish. And once we get rolling, we can lose perspective and just push ahead. It's easier to charge forward than it is to back off. Besides, sometimes we want to win because we know we *can*, not necessarily because we *should*.

One SWW describes her struggle with anger this way: "How can I keep the will to make changes and fight what's wrong (or just ridiculous) if I'm *not* angry? As a kid I would get mad at the thought that time would dissipate my anger, because it felt like my will was draining away with it. I hated being sent to my room and not being able to fight to the finish. I would vow to stay mad until I could finish the fight. I still feel that to some extent."

AWARENESS IS HALF THE BATTLE

You might identify with the SWW who admitted, "Back me in the corner and I come out fighting. I use all my knowledge to back myself up. I attempt to listen to the other person; however, I know I'm too busy thinking of what I'm going to say next. When I feel I'm right, it will take a lot to change my mind."

There are occasions when, without even thinking, your first reaction is to strike back and retaliate with a swift and brutal retort—and the progression to a meltdown can be swift and irreversible. I compare it to the chain of events that leads to the release of nuclear warheads. Once the confrontation has started, it's almost impossible to turn back.

Most of us don't like this side of our strong will. It's harder to control, and it can have serious consequences when it comes to our relationships. I know I've wished many times that I could just let it go when I see myself heading for disaster in an argument. The Lord is still working with me, and through the years I've become much better at choosing my battles. Even now there are times when I let that nuclear sequence begin and I know the countdown clock is ticking.

Here are a few of the most common trigger phrases that can set a nuclear battle in motion when directed toward an SWW. I'm sure you can add your own to the list.

- "That's just not going to happen."
- "Calm down."
- "Don't be so sensitive."
- "It must be nice to know it all."
- "You just want to have everything your own way."
- "You've got a bad attitude."
- "What's your problem?"
- "Is it that time of month again?"

Awareness *is* half the battle. If we recognize what's happening, we have a first line of defense, and before we strike, we can put into motion a plan to avoid a total meltdown. Here are a few suggestions for how we can respond to a trigger phrase:

- "I'm going to pretend you didn't just say that. I need a couple minutes." Then walk away if it helps you keep your composure.
- "Are you *trying* to make me mad at you?"
- "You're kidding, right?"
- "Is that really what you want to ask me?"
- You could use a code word—something you and the other person have agreed to ahead of time. For example, "Ouch." When either you or the person who's talking to you sense the conversation is starting to go sideways, saying "Ouch" can give you a chance to stop and reconsider before an argument escalates.

You can come up with other alternatives that work for your own situations. The important thing is that you recognize what sets you off and that you consciously work on breaking the pattern of automatically responding without thinking.

Kym wrote a note in her survey about how she handles this issue: "I really try to be honest with myself and realize that I can usually get my way, but it will come at a cost. The end result is pain for me and others. For the most part, I have learned to submit my stubborn objectives to God and even surrender things I truly desire when I believe fully they are opposite of His desire for me—at least for the most part!"

Holding back when we'd rather let loose isn't something we can consistently do under our own power. But in the hands of the Holy Spirit, our strong will can be a credit to the One who designed it. He can help us focus our strong will on the situations where we can make a positive impact, then leave the others to Him.

INTEGRITY IN UNGUARDED MOMENTS

If we're living all out for God, our motivation and actions will be in line with His Word. Our desire to conquer takes a backseat to our desire to keep our life in line with His will and to bring Him honor. Philippians 1:27 tells us to "live in such a way that you are a credit to the Message of Christ." None of us will get it right every time. All of us will occasionally fail under stress or pure frustration. But the bottom line is this: it is our heart's desire to live in a way that reflects Christ. One SWW admits, "Being strong willed is tough. It is a constant battle of not giving up, but not going too far. You have to know when to pull back, and you have to constantly look to God to let you know when a battle is worth it, no matter how hard you have to push."

When we keep that goal foremost in our minds, we can direct our strong will to the task of practicing restraint in the face of conflict and confrontation, and discipline ourselves to look for the path that uses our strength to do the most good.

Most of us aren't tempted by obvious sins. If we're given too much change at a store, we return it. If we're not charged for an item, we take it back to the store and pay for it. We would not report more hours than we worked. We wouldn't cheat on our taxes. We know that everything we say and do matters to God, especially when it comes to morality and ethics.

But even the most godly SWW can be tempted to use her innate abilities to manipulate circumstances to achieve her goals. We find out at a young age that we have a knack for finding loopholes when we're looking for a way to get around a pesky rule or avoid obeying what we consider to be an unreasonable edict from an authority figure. One SWW—we'll call her Connie—shares how she used her manipulative talent when she was a new teacher working for a very authoritarian department head—we'll call him Ron. Connie was a popular teacher with her students, which seemed to irritate Ron and some of the other teachers. One day at lunch, Ron told Connie she needed to use a specific textbook with her students.

Connie objected. "Ron, that book is on the supplemental textbook list, and I already have a full schedule of lessons without it."

Ron glared at her and pointed his finger in her face. "I'm your supervisor, and I'm telling you that you're going to use that textbook. Do you understand me?"

Connie's eyes narrowed, and she pursed her lips. "Sure. Fine."

After lunch Connie went to the book room and got a stack

of the textbooks Ron had decreed she must use. She asked all her students to stand at their desks as she handed out the books. Then she instructed the students to place the book on the seat of their chairs and sit down—on the books.

"Just trust me," she said when she saw their quizzical looks.

After her students left the classroom, Connie gathered all the books and returned them to the book room. A few days later Ron cornered her and asked smugly if she had used the textbooks he told her to use. She smiled and said, "Yes, Ron, we did use those books. Thanks for your suggestion." And she walked away.

Connie still claims that if Ron had asked her *how* she used them, she would have been honest with him. But looking back now as a more mature SWW, Connie admits it wasn't the right thing to do. She got by on a technicality, but it revealed a weakness in her integrity.

My SWW friend Sue says she likes to consider herself "charmingly manipulative" when it comes to dealing with people like Ron. Another friend says, "I sometimes end up feeling foolish for having dug in so hard. I'm determined until I get my way, then I feel terribly guilty when I win. I feel sad for the person I 'conquered.'" However you look at it, it's important to recognize how easy it is to let our natural talent for getting around a troublesome rule become a situation where we aren't a credit to the message of Christ.

THE POWER OF GRACE

Another theme that often comes up when talking to SWWs is our frequent inability to hide our impatience with people or situations that exasperate us. Most of us admit that the way we express our frustration can get the desired results, but the cost is often damage to a relationship. Kathleen, an SWW from my survey, tells how her actions in unguarded moments affect others:

> The Lord teaches me valuable lessons in humility and puts
> me in a position of needing to humble myself, pray, and go
> to those whom I have offended, say I was wrong, and ask
> for forgiveness. I do not tell others I am sorry, because in
> my heart, if I am honest, I am probably not sorry a bit. But
> if I am wrong about something, that's an entirely different
> story. I need to own up to whatever it is that took me to
> the dark side of being strong willed and admit to the Lord,
> to others, and to myself that what I did was wrong and
> seek forgiveness and restoration.

Many of us find that our greatest difficulties are with those closest to us. But we can easily fall into the habit of being impatient with almost anyone. We lead busy lives and when we're in a hurry, our patience often takes a backseat. But if the desire of our heart is to honor God, we know our attitude and actions make a big difference. Actor, producer, and SWW Roma Downey has great wisdom on how to avoid running over others when we're trying to accomplish something: "I have learned that between stimulus and response there is a space. I like to call it a space of grace. I make my best decisions from that space."[1]

We strengthen our integrity and character when we take a moment before we react to something so the Holy Spirit has a chance to insert His wisdom. When we get frustrated with a slow-moving cashier at the grocery store, for instance, we choose to remind ourselves to be kind. If a service employee is not being friendly or helpful, we choose to assume that perhaps she received bad news earlier in the day. We choose to give her the benefit of the doubt, to understand that we do not see the full picture. And so we choose to give her grace.

We have the power to cut down or to build up—and we can do either in an instant. Often we look at situations and decide we can step in and get the job done quicker than anyone else. While that may be true, it may not be for the best. We can move things forward and get things going and solve almost everyone's problems. But here's the question we need to ask ourselves: Just because we can do it, does it mean we should?

YVETTE MAHER

Yvette Maher grew up in Lincoln County, Kentucky, where thoroughbred horses are abundant. Thoroughbreds are hot-blooded animals, known for their agility, speed, and spirit. They are bred to run. When thoroughbreds race, they perform with maximum exertion—just as many women of strong will do and just as Yvette does. On a scale of one to twelve for how intense a strong-willed personality she has, she ranks about a ten.

Yvette claims to have gotten her strong will honestly:

> Grandma Thelma left the female Greers [Yvette's
> maiden name] a legacy: a double-edged sword.
> On one edge of the sword was the ability to
> accomplish tasks quickly and efficiently. That
> skill set was certainly needed on the farm with
> the variety of daily chores; Grandma's being well
> organized and capable was often the difference
> between eating or starving. The other side of the
> sword was a bossy personality. Grandma Thelma
> was a strong-willed, weather-beaten country

woman who moved along at a fast, clicking pace. Everything was always in motion. Everything was planned. Everything was accomplished. She gave commands.[2]

The women in Yvette's family inherited the controlling tone (or "gift," as they like to say). If people listened for it, they could recognize certain undertones conveying, for example, *I'm right and you're wrong* and *You better get out of the way 'cause I'm comin' through.* That tone could also say, *I don't need your opinion. You're dead weight and holding me back!*

Yvette knew that she needed to be careful of the way she commented to others and that she could build up or destroy her relationships with her tone. "We must take our passions and desires and humbly rein in the gift of will God has given us," she said. "We must put it under His control. We have to take the bit in our mouth and wear the bridle of restraint that He has for us. Then He can use us for the purposes He has intended—strong will and all."

The biggest problem for Yvette when it comes to her strong will is her unmet expectations. "It's the walking out, confronting, facing, and dealing with them. I suppose I thought that if I could control a situation, it would go the way I expected. But life's not like that." She learned that truth the hard way when she was sixteen and her parents divorced. "I thought we were a happy family," she said. But when her family dissolved, she took her own wayward path and soon found herself unwed and pregnant. Not knowing any better at the time, she had an abortion. "None of what happened was what I expected."

Later she fell genuinely in love and married. She became pregnant and gave birth to twin daughters. About that time she also found Jesus. Since all those wonderful things had happened, she figured her life and happiness were set. "I thought all my unmet expectations were about to be met and life was going to be happy."

But it didn't turn out the way she anticipated. Her dad spent ten years in prison for killing his third wife's lover. After being released from prison, he later shot his girlfriend, then turned the gun on himself. Fortunately, he survived the wounds, but he is serving a life-plus sentence. Her uncle walked into an elementary school and shot and killed his wife, who was the school secretary, then killed himself.

Then the troubles visited her own family. In 2008 her husband, Tommy, exploded after a major verbal fight with Yvette. He yelled, "I'm done. I won't be under your thumb any longer. You're not going to disrespect me."[3] And with that, he asked for a separation.

"I had yet to learn that my strength comes from the Lord and that I must run to Him," she said. "I'm trying to learn how to make the distance to Him a lot shorter." That includes what she says and the tone she communicates.

She and Tommy reconciled. They have now been married twenty-seven years and their children are grown. Her professional life got on track as well. She is now executive pastor at New Life Church in Colorado Springs where ten thousand people worship. She oversees the women's and children's ministries, the fifty-plus ministry, and the small-group ministry. She is also an author, speaker, podcast director, and she has served as a vice president at Focus on the Family.

She's learned that nothing is impossible with God. "Considering the life I lived, the choices I made, I am amazed that He allows me to utter His name, to love selflessly, to openly share my story, and to forgive wholeheartedly, much less allow me to minister for Him. I have no credentials for the work I have done and am doing. Yet God has seen fit to provide the pathway on which I walk."

Yvette's life has been filled with crazy, inexplicable, fear-filled life events, yet she has been showered with God's grace and mercy. While she has matured, she still struggles with her strong will. "I picture [God] looking down at me, when I've exerted my strong will and hurt someone or made them angry, and saying, *Really, Stubborn Head, are we going to do this again?* I feel that He allows me to say, 'I blew it. It was my strong will, my opinions, what I thought.' I have to ask myself, *Is this God's will or my strong will? Just how am I applying the will that God gave me?*"

One important lesson she's learned is that we need to study humility and embrace it. She understands that sometimes our strong, beautiful will can get us into situations we don't want to be in and it can take us places we don't want to go.

And those hot-blooded thoroughbreds she grew up near? She's learned another lesson from them: the best way to rein in our strong will is to bridle ourselves.

She explains that horses have to be put into a headstall (a bridle) that holds a bit in place in their mouths. Because the reins are attached to the bit, the slightest pressure on the reins from the rider is directed to the horse's mouth so it knows what is expected. Some horses are put into a bitless bridle called a hackamore. The rider directs the horse with the slightest pressure to the hackamore's noseband. Hackamores can only be used with a horse who knows its rider so well that when it feels the slightest pressure on sensitive areas of the face where the hackamore touches, it is enough to provide direction and control.

We probably don't have to state the obvious point of this comparison, but we will. The strong-willed woman is the thoroughbred in the bridle. Will she need a bit, or can she be put in a hackamore? Will she be so sensitive to God's leading that only the slightest pressure from Him will be necessary to direct her?

For her own strong will, Yvette uses what she calls a "grace pace," which allows her to stop, bridle herself, and walk toward what is ahead of her. If instead, we run ahead in zeal and passion like the thoroughbred horse, which can run till its heart bursts, we may end up running ahead of God. We may not have the maturity to support our zeal and passion, and that will be hurtful to us, as well as to others.

Thoroughbred horses are bred to run the narrow boundary of the racetrack. If a thoroughbred is turned loose on a street—say in a parade—it will create chaos and possibly hurt someone. In our strong-willed passion for this life, we have to know the boundaries.

What does it mean to be bridled and have a bit in our mouth? What does it mean to humbly submit to the Lord, to follow His lead, to stay within the boundaries He has set?

When Yvette looks back over her life and considers how her strong will has become a huge asset, she knows it's because she's practiced allowing God to bridle her. As 2 Timothy 2:21 (her favorite verse) reminds us: "If you keep yourself pure, you will be a special utensil for honorable use. Your life will be clean, and you will be ready for the Master to use you for every good work" (NLT). It's wisdom worth acknowledging.

DIRECTING OUR **PASSION** AND DEFINING OUR *Purpose*

The television reporter interviewed participants at one of the training centers for the Centers for Disease Control (CDC) on how to deal with Ebola victims. It had been less than a week since an Ebola patient had died in a Dallas hospital, and the whole country was on high alert. While most of those being trained were from local hospitals and clinics, a few represented Samaritan's Purse, an international Christian relief organization, and they were headed to West Africa—ground zero for the deadly virus.

The journalist approached one of the nurses and asked why

in the world she would choose to go right into the center of that disease-ridden country, knowing it could mean certain death. The nurse gave her reply calmly and with a smile. "We're just being the hands and feet of Jesus." The reporter shook his head in disbelief and asked the nurse next to her the same question. She gave essentially the same answer, then added, "I asked my family for their support, but not their permission. I know what God is calling me to do, and I must do it."

SWWs understand this degree of passion and purpose better than anyone else. We've been given great gifts of determination, strength, and will. We tend to stand out. We understand that our purpose can't be taken lightly. We realize that when we dedicate our strong will to God, we choose to represent Him, to fulfill His plan, to be His hands and feet—even if it costs us everything.

Not every SWW will be called to serve in dangerous and extreme conditions. We may not have a high-profile position or a grand and glorious profession. Not everyone will need to be a flashy public speaker or a famous film star in order to fulfill God's purpose. But we are all critical to His plan, and He uses our wide variety of personalities and strengths to accomplish amazing things. One thing is certain: the chances are good that SWWs will rock the boat more often than they will sit quietly and simply row in rhythm with the others on board.

I like what Brennan Manning writes in *The Signature of*

Jesus about how God uses us and our gifts to fulfill His purposes:

> One of the stunning lessons of the Bible is God's free use
> of fragile human beings to accomplish his purpose. He
> does not always choose the holy and devout or even the
> emotionally well-balanced. . . . "The Holy Spirit is the
> bearer of gifts and these gifts are sometimes lavished in
> peculiar places." God bestows his grace abundantly but
> unevenly. He offers no explanation why some are called
> to radical discipleship and others are not.[1]

SWWs don't usually struggle with uncertainty when it comes to what we want to do. In fact, when faced with a fork in the road, it's much more likely we'll make a poor decision than no decision at all. And therein lies the challenge. There's no shortage of causes, no lack of opportunities to use our strong will with passion and drive. But it's important that we also be focused on making sure we're following *God's* plan and not just chasing our own ideas. On her survey, Arlyn put it this way: "I tend to take action even if I'm not completely confident I know what I'm doing. I would rather do something wrong (and fix it later) than do nothing at all."

Of course it would be a lot easier if God just had some sort of quick and clear message system to communicate His plans for us. Every SWW knows that life is full of possibilities—lots of them—and we're pretty sure we could do anything we really set our minds to. But how can we be sure we'll recognize which plan is God's—and by the way, doesn't it feel like we should be doing something to move things along?

Unfortunately, as we've already discussed in previous chapters, He doesn't quite work that way. But we keep getting tempted just to forge ahead, don't we? That's why I like the reminder that Oswald Chambers offers us:

> God does not tell you what He is going to do; He reveals to you Who He is. Do you believe in a miracle-working God, and will you go out in surrender to Him until you are not surprised an atom at anything He does?[2] . . . There are times when you cannot understand why you cannot do what you want to do. When God brings the blank space, see that you do not fill it in, but wait.[3]

When I stop telling God what I want, He can fill me in on what He wants without my own plans getting in the way.

GOD KNOWS WHAT HE'S DOING WITH US

The better we get to know God, the easier it is to trust that whatever comes our way is part of His plan for us. Even SWWs can practice resting and waiting for Him to show us the next step, knowing He has only our best interests at heart.

In September 1971, I packed my bags and left my home in Las Vegas (where my dad was pastoring) to begin my freshman year of college in Idaho—a huge change of scenery for this city girl. The first afternoon I was there, I walked to the center of campus and stopped at the foot of the clock tower. As I looked up at the clock, I reminded God about my lifelong dream.

"I want to be a writer," I said out loud. Then I added silently, *Maybe the editor of a famous New York magazine. I'll do whatever I have to do to get there, God. Except become a teacher. That's too boring. I'll do anything but teach.*

Halfway through my freshman year, I became acutely aware that I was at a college that was nationally renowned for its education program and outstanding teachers, and I surrendered to what felt like an unmistakable push toward getting a degree in teaching.

"Okay," I told God, "but not in Idaho. It's out in the middle of farm country. That's too boring. I'll teach anywhere but Idaho."

It won't surprise you that, after graduating, I spent three years teaching at a public high school in Idaho. Throughout my college years, I had to learn to listen to God's voice and willingly lay down my own will to follow what I knew was God's path for me. Those experiences taught my strong-willed heart two important truths: (1) Don't tell God what you will and won't do, and (2) It's easier than I thought to fall in love with Idaho!

I loved teaching high school, and I was determined to be unlike any teacher those students had ever had before. They loved my unconventional methods, creative lesson ideas, and total dedication to my work, but in spite of all that, I discovered that most students were frustrated, bored, and unchallenged by school in general. I began a passionate search for keys to unlock the potential in what I was sure were future world changers. Every summer I went back to work in "the real world," not only to stay diverse in my skills and training, but also to find out how I could help my students prepare for success after their classroom education. I chauffeured limousines, worked for the Mack Trucks manufacturing company, inventoried slot machine parts in Las Vegas, and did a variety of office jobs. I quickly realized that most people get hired for the things they got in trouble for in school—good social interaction, independent thinking skills, high energy level. That knowledge and experience fueled and intensified my search for a way to change the way we educate all students—and I was convinced I could find the means to do it.

After three years of teaching, I moved from Idaho to Washington State and taught in an urban public high school. During my first summer something happened to change my life again. I took a ride-along with a police officer friend, and I was hooked. I knew I had to be a cop, at least for a while.

Although I wasn't ready to quit teaching, I applied and was accepted as a volunteer in the police officer reserve program. As a fully commissioned reserve officer in the city of Des Moines, just south of Seattle, for six years I worked part time (evenings and weekends) during the school year and almost full time during the summers. It didn't take long for the police department to tap into my teaching skills to help train other new officers, and I was surprised to find that mature adults shared the same learning challenges as my high school students.

About that time, Seattle Pacific University (SPU) hosted a weekend seminar with a leading educational expert and primary researcher who specialized in the field of *learning styles,* the inborn strengths and preferences we all possess and how we can use them to learn and succeed. SPU was offering a master's degree with learning styles as a specialty, so I immediately signed up for the program. As I worked on my graduate degree, I also began teaching educator and parenting seminars about these exciting and encouraging concepts.

I got married during that time, and then in April 1991, I gave birth to twin sons, Michael and Robert, born two minutes apart. From the beginning they looked like Pete and Re-Pete, but it was immediately evident that they were opposite in personality and learning style. God had given me my very own in-home laboratory!

I had a wide variety of experience—in business, law enforcement, teaching, and adult education—but nothing compared to the new world that opened to me as a mom. Now my theories and strategies were put to the test in the most important arena of all—and if I could make them work there, I believed I just might be able to change the world after all.

Late in 1992, I got a phone call from Gwen Ellis, who at that time was an editor at Focus on the Family in Colorado Springs. She told me that one of their authors had attended a learning styles seminar I taught in Seattle and had been so enthusiastic about it that he brought Focus the handouts from the class. She paused and said, "We loved the material. And we're wondering if you would be interested in writing a book for us?"

I replied breathlessly, "Let-me-think-about-it-yes!"

My life was about to change forever again.

It was a new and fascinating adventure to write a book, and Gwen was my mentor and shepherd all the way through. That book, *The Way They Learn,* was released in October 1994—almost twenty-three years to the day when I had stood at the foot of the campus clock tower and told God that all I wanted to be was a writer. I could imagine Him smiling as He asked, *What would you have written about back then?*

Of course, if I had known at the age of eighteen that it would take more than twenty years to see my dream of being a writer come true, it would have been terribly discouraging. But that's not how God works. He weaves our experiences and detours along the journey into a wonderful tapestry that serves as the perfect background for what He has planned. As an SWW, I sometimes forget that it's not God who is like me; it's me who needs to be more like Him. We were created in *His* image, not the other way around. His ways and His thoughts are not ours.[4] And neither is His timetable.

My story is not unique—every SWW could write a whole book on how her passions and interests have been taken down unexpected paths by the God who knows how to use her strengths to accomplish His will and purpose.

OUR JOY IN PURSUING GOD'S PURPOSE

Will we find our greatest happiness when we discover God's purpose for our lives? Psychologist Dr. Larry Crabb makes an interesting distinction between the word *happiness* and the word *joy.* Although he agrees that happiness can come from getting the right things, he reminds us that joy is what happens when you can be happy even when life doesn't turn out the way you planned: "I believe that joy is available to anybody at any time in any circumstance and any condition of soul, if you define joy not as dependent on what you get from another but what you give to another that God has given you—the commitment to the well-being of another at any cost to yourself. When you relate like that, you'll know what the word *joy* means."[5]

I can think of many SWWs who are wonderful examples of that definition of joy, and I'm inspired by how they let God use them—even when they never dreamed how the tapestry of their lives would look when He was finished.

One of those SWWs is Corrie ten Boom, who was born April 15, 1892, in the Netherlands. She was the daughter of a jeweler and watchmaker, and she traveled an extraordinarily difficult path that would reveal to the world just what a woman of great strength and purpose she was. Corrie's heart was broken by her mother's death and then again by a failed romance. But God was working with her to change the happiness she thought she wanted into the joy of becoming His instrument for changing the world in ways she couldn't have dreamed. She started her new direction by studying to help her father in his business. Her interest and aptitude resulted in a record-breaking achievement: in 1922 she became the first woman in Holland to be officially licensed as a watchmaker.

Eighteen years later, in May 1940, World War II and God gave Corrie the greatest challenge any strong-willed woman can imagine. Not only was Corrie going to save hundreds of Jewish lives, but she would do it by constantly risking her own. For many it is a familiar story told in Corrie's book *The Hiding Place*. She and her family built a secret room no bigger than a closet behind a false wall in Corrie's bedroom. If everyone who hid in the closet stood very close together and stayed totally quiet, this tiny room would save their lives from the Nazis. Corrie embraced this risk, to the point that she ended up overseeing an entire network of similar safe houses before the war was over.

Early in 1944 the Nazis arrested the ten Boom family, and Corrie and her sister Betsie spent the rest of that year in the Ravensbrück concentration camp. Betsie died in December 1944, just twelve days before Corrie was released. Instead of getting some rest and taking time to recover, Corrie immediately set up a rehabilitation center for concentration camp survivors.

In 1946 she began a worldwide ministry that lasted until a series of strokes in 1978 left her unable to speak. Was this what Corrie had initially pictured her life would be? Most likely not, yet it's impossible to know how many lives she saved by her courageous actions or how many souls have been uplifted by her books and writings over the decades. We can find an underlying thread on the tapestry of Corrie's life in a small but profound phrase she penned: "Joy runs deeper than despair."

There is a traditional Jewish belief that only specially blessed people are granted the privilege of dying on the date they were born. In 1983, at the age of ninety-one, Corrie ten Boom died on April 15—her birthday. God used her strong will in amazing ways—but I feel certain He led her down a path she would not have designed for herself.

Another of my favorite inspirational SWWs is Elisabeth Elliot. She and her husband, Jim, followed God's will and the vision to be missionaries to the savage Auca tribe in the primitive jungles of Ecuador. When their daughter was just ten months old, Jim was tragically killed by members of that tribe, and Elisabeth became a widow after only three years of marriage. Instead of retreating to safety and comfort, she stayed in the mission field of Ecuador with her daughter for several more years, living with and continuing to minister to the very tribe that had killed her husband.

Many years later, she was asked to host a fifteen-minute radio program for Back to the Bible, and she began each talk this way: "You are loved with an everlasting love. That's what the Bible says—and underneath are the Everlasting Arms." After losing so many years of happiness she could have known with her husband, she gained the kind of deep fulfillment that comes only from being in the center of God's will. The name of her radio program? *Gateway to Joy.*[6]

If we're living for God, it's not about us at all. Since we're part of a much bigger picture, we must continually search for, know, and pursue His purpose. Instead of laying out our own plans for His approval, we submit to the beautiful tapestry He's designed to fulfill *His* plans. And as Corrie and Elisabeth have shown us, that's what changes the world.

WHAT IF IT'S YOU?

In all things great and small, we've been given the incredible privilege of being a blessing to others, answering the prayers of strangers, and making a difference in the world just by following Jesus. Though that can be said of everyone who follows Christ, as SWWs, we have an even higher standard: "From everyone to whom much has been given, much will be required; and from the one to whom much has been entrusted, even more will be demanded" (Luke 12:48, NRSV).

What vision has God given you? What is He saying to you right now? It may not be a mission call to the ends of the earth, or an international ministry, or even a life of full-time Christian service. But what if you're the one who is supposed to sound the call to action—gather the support, motivate, inspire, teach, preach, serve? What if it's your voice the world is waiting to hear?

Lynne Hybels, published author and the wife of Bill Hybels, founding pastor of Willow Creek Community Church in the Chicago suburbs, admits it took her way too long to come to the realization that God had called her for a specific purpose—and she struggled with feeling qualified to answer. She writes:

> It was years before I learned to value myself enough to believe that God's call on my life was something I had to take seriously. . . . There was a perspective and a dream— there were words and influence—that I believe God wanted me to offer to my church. But I didn't show up. I didn't value what I had to offer enough to actually offer it. . . .
>
> I believe that too many women give bits and pieces of themselves away, indiscriminately, for years and years, and never have the time or energy to discern their unique calling from God, never have the time or energy to play the redemptive role they are gifted and impassioned to play. The result is a lot of good-hearted, devout Christian women who are exhausted and depressed.[7]

Is that you? Are you holding back from what you know God wants you to pursue? If so, can you imagine what you— and others—are missing because of that choice?

You Always Make a Difference

Even if you don't deliberately set out to influence others, when you're an SWW you're going to affect those around you, whether or not you intend to.

David, one of my colleagues, was flying cross-country and found that his seatmate was a new mother holding an infant. But this was not your typical mom. This young mother had been born with no arms. David watched with fascination as she balanced her baby between the stubs of her upper arms and her very agile feet. Finally, halfway through the flight, he couldn't resist asking her, "I'm sorry if this seems rude, but I just have to know. Don't you find it incredibly hard to take care of a baby when you have no arms?"

She smiled. "Well, there is one big disadvantage." When he looked puzzled, she said, "Watch." Swiftly, with her feet, she reached into the diaper bag and got a bottle of formula. Then expertly with her feet, she put it in her infant's mouth. Instantly the baby took hold of the bottle with his feet, his arms lying motionless at his sides. She turned to David. "He doesn't know he has arms yet, because he's never seen me use mine."

Like this young mother, we make a significant impression on those around us, and our words and actions are often imitated, even if we don't intend them to be. We don't get to choose whether or not we affect others. We *do* influence them, in large ways and small.

As an SWW, the reality is that God definitely wants to use you to accomplish something special and important. That doesn't always mean it will be earthshaking or even noticeable to more than a few people. But when you step out in faith and follow your vision and call from God, others will pay attention—so be sure it's His purpose and plan you're pursuing.

PROFILES IN
Perseverance

JANINE MAXWELL

Janine Maxwell ran for her life while a policeman shouted, "Get out of the building. There's a bomb in Grand Central Station!" The date was September 11, 2001. The place was New York City.

Janine, a successful CEO of her own business, Onyx Marketing Group, in Canada, was in New York attending the Marketing to Kids seminar. She, along with so many others, stood in the train station waiting for the day to begin and watching TV when the newsflash came that the World Trade Center had been hit by a plane. Minutes later she saw a second plane smash into the second Trade Center tower.

Even though it turned out there was no bomb in Grand Central Station, people fled for their lives, Janine among them—hiking in high heels away from lower Manhattan in hopes of finding a safer place. No one knew for sure where that safer place might be. Janine's husband, Ian, was in Chicago on business that day, and when all flights were canceled and the Canadian border closed, he, like so many others, was trapped in the United States. Days later, after unbelievable struggles, they both made their way home. That day, when America was attacked, changed the world. And that day also changed Janine's life forever.

Once home, she became anxious and depressed. She spent weeks in bed trying to recover from the trauma she had seen on the television and had experienced personally through the chaos of trying to escape—images of falling bodies, a dazed man covered in white dust walking north out of the city, burning buildings, and the overwhelming terror that she or her husband might never get home to their children. The world had gone mad, and there was nothing she could do to control anything. She installed a TV set in every room in her house and in her office so that she could be continually vigilant. She would keep guard to make sure that she could control something: to keep her loved ones safe. But fear overwhelmed her life. Slowly, with medical help, time, books, and the Word of God, she began to understand that God had a new purpose for her life.

About a year and a half after 9/11, she was invited to fill in for a guest who couldn't make it to an appearance on *100 Huntley Street,* a popular Christian show on Canadian television. Seated next to her was an old college friend she hadn't seen in years. She began to chat with him and get reacquainted. During their conversation, she learned that he had been working in Africa filming street kids. He explained that there are thousands of kids all over Africa whose parents have died and left them alone and with no resources. Here was something new and exciting to distract her. When she expressed her interest in going with him and his wife to Africa, he immediately invited her to go on his next trip, which happened to be in just four weeks. She jumped at the opportunity and soon found herself on a plane bound for Zambia.

When she first got there, she had little to do but sit and observe, and observe she did. All of a sudden, another world, one she'd never paid much attention to before, filled her sight, mind, spirit, and senses. One night on that trip, Janine found her purpose. There on the streets of Lusaka, Zambia's capital city, she saw piles of garbage suddenly move and little heads poke out of them—street children. They were dirty, hungry, and alone with no one to love and care for them, and they huddled close together under garbage to keep warm. When she asked about them, her friend explained that there were seventy-five thousand of these children on the streets of Zambia alone.

The numbers overwhelmed her and she began to consider, *What about the rest of Africa? What about*

God? What kind of God allows this to happen? What kind of God sits back and lets His kids be treated worse than animals? The thoughts plagued her. She couldn't sleep, she couldn't think straight, and she struggled to breathe.

Something had to be done—and right away.

Janine returned home a changed person. She had no heart left for her thriving business. For a while she went through the motions and continued serving as president of the company, but it was no use. Her heart was in Africa. So she began to travel back to Africa, expanding her trips to other countries—Malawi, Kenya, and Swaziland.

As her purpose became clearer, she shared with her husband, Ian, about what God was doing in her life. He had little interest, however. So Janine prayed and waited for God to speak to Ian. Soon, Ian heard God's call too, and they closed the business and turned their lives in a whole new direction: service to those who have nothing.[8]

Today Janine and Ian head up Heart for Africa, a faith-based organization that focuses on bringing hope to the people of Africa, working specifically in the areas of hunger, poverty, education, and the care of orphans. And just a few years ago through a series of miracles that read like the book of Acts, they purchased a 2,500-acre farm and called it Project Canaan. It is there that Swazis find work, acceptance, and hope as they farm to provide food for the homeless, which include more than 200,000 Swazi orphans. Thanks to Janine's strong-willed spirit, she wasn't content to stop there. She also started a home for orphan babies who were sick and abandoned. Now several dozen babies are thriving at Project Canaan Children.

Janine, like the apostle Paul, had an encounter that completely shifted the direction of her life. She could have ignored the whole experience. She could have walked away from the cries of thousands upon thousands of orphaned African children. She could have continued to make the big bucks at her agency rather than live halfway around the world where crocodiles and snakes and hail and storms and heat and disease and cold are day-to-day realities. But she didn't. She took the strength of her character, her ability as a fund-raiser and marketer, and her strong will, and she put them to work for the children of Swaziland. She moved to a farm and learned to pray for rain to fill the pond behind their dam. She learned that when storms flatten every living thing in sight, you pull yourself up and start a campaign to bring in the needed money to begin the recovery.

This is a woman who will accomplish what she's been given to do. She will raise the money again and again to further the work. She will find a place to tuck in one more baby. She will trust God to care for her now almost-grown children living in the far-flung corners of the earth. She is the epitome of strong will used in a way that brings honor and glory to God.

LEADERSHIP
WITH
Integrity

When my third child was only five years old, we asked her what she wanted to be when she grew up. Without missing a beat, she said, 'In charge.' She meant it!"

Amy's description of her strong-willed daughter could describe almost every SWW. Like it or not, if you're an SWW, you have a persistent and irresistible urge to step up and take charge in almost any situation. Although there are times when it can earn you the label of "bossy," strong will can also provide you with the courage and boldness to stay calm in a crisis, and help you bring order out of chaos.

Although SWWs are diverse, as Christians we share a common bond when it comes to our desire to use that strong will in ways that honor God when we do take charge. That sounds a lot easier than it is—because prioritizing God means leading with a servant's heart. As Paul reminded us in Philippians 2:3–4, "In humility value others above yourselves, not looking to your own interests but each of you to the interests of the others" (NIV). And as noted English evangelical leader John Stott further explained, "The authority by which the Christian leader leads is not power but love, not force but example, not coercion but reasoned persuasion. Leaders have power, but power is safe only in the hands of those who humble themselves to serve."[1]

Sometimes your strong will has to step up in big ways. Sometimes it has to stand toe-to-toe with evil or pray down strongholds of the Enemy. But a strong will consecrated to God produces strength of spirit, clear-eyed purpose, and deep compassion that works in small and daily ways as well.

This leadership takes a myriad of forms. A stay-at-home mom and a high-level executive may share similar leadership qualities—but use them in different ways. When it comes to influence, a mom shares the same responsibility for the effect her leadership has on her children as the corporate executive does for how her leadership impacts her employees. Every SWW—married, single, divorced, widowed, working inside or outside the home, corporate executive, or community volunteer—will be called to lead in some way.

Meg shares what works for her in her leadership, both in the business world and at home: "Over the years I've learned to avoid demanding my own way. Instead, I persuade by building vision with hope and drive, and by using enthusiasm, examples, and unavoidable conclusions. I outwit those who stand in the way and get them to think it is their idea to change!"

Regardless of where we use our leadership gifts, it's important to remember to do so with integrity and a servant's heart.

WHAT MAKES SWW LEADERSHIP SO SPECIAL?

There's a significant difference when an SWW's leadership honors God as first priority. It goes against what the world insists women who want to be in charge need to do in order to be successful. Consider these differences:

The world says: "Take a moment now to think about the most important people in your life. What do they get from *you*? What do you get from *them*? Is the exchange equitable? If you feel as if you're giving more than you're getting, then you're being swindled."[2]

But Jesus says: "Give, and you will receive. Your gift will return to you in full—pressed down, shaken together to make room for more, running over, and poured into your lap. The amount you give will determine the amount you get back."—Luke 6:38, NLT

The world says: "The techniques and advice given here will help any working woman to claim what she wants and what is hers. . . . 'Someone once told me that when she got promoted she received a letter from another female executive. It said, *"Behind every woman who gets promoted is herself."*'"3

But Jesus says: "'If you want to claim credit, claim it for God.' What you say about yourself means nothing in God's work. It's what God says about you that makes the difference."—2 Corinthians 10:17–18

When SWWs live all out for God, no matter what we do or where we serve, our highest goal is to lift up Christ, to reflect His nature and behavior. Others will often imitate us, so we must be sure we are imitating Christ. Second Corinthians 3:3 reminds us: "Your very lives are a letter that anyone can read by just looking at you. Christ himself wrote it—not with ink, but with God's living Spirit; not chiseled into stone, but carved into human lives—and we publish it."

As SWWs who consistently seek to serve others and to bring honor and glory to God, our work ethic, our integrity, and our mission will all be reflections of Christ and His love. Amy shares how this truth works in her career: "Seeking God first and being willing to submit to His principles sometimes doesn't seem to make good business sense. But when I follow God's leading in a world that's His creation, His design— amazingly enough, it works."

No One Said It Would Be Easy

Of course, if it were *easy* to lead like this, everyone would do it. But like everything in an SWW's life, Christlike leadership presents some tall challenges, and none of us gets it right every time. The businesswomen in my survey all admitted that strong will can present its greatest difficulties when it comes to getting along with those we lead. I remember seeing someone wear a T-shirt that read "Teamwork is everyone doing it my way." I smiled, but I have to admit I've caught myself operating that way sometimes. We do often have to make a conscious effort to keep our strong will from taking its natural course when we're confident we already know what to do.

You might be encouraged to see just a few examples of survey statements I believe we can all identify with on this topic of leadership:

- "It's hard to know when to keep my mouth shut—especially when I know something needs to change or something's not right. I have to exercise great self-control."
- "I can fall into being combative when I face opposition. It's hard to back down."
- "I can come across as bossy, and I have trouble relating to people who need to be led step by step."

I think my favorite comment was this one: "I can cheerfully steamroll over people!" Ouch. Doesn't sound too Christlike, does it? That's why it's important that we don't try to lead from our own strength, and why we must continually listen to the Holy Spirit and what He tells us to do.

STAYING ACCOUNTABLE

We know we need to stay close to God through prayer and reading His Word—but there's another step we can take that isn't quite as straightforward: allowing others to hold us accountable. It's important to identify at least two or three close, trusted friends or colleagues who are willing to be our accountability partners.

These are people to whom we give not only permission, but also the responsibility to keep us aware of our words and actions. If they see us do something, or hear us say something, that calls into question our integrity or in any way compromises our representation of Christ, it's their duty to pull us aside and talk to us about it. We agree ahead of time to listen carefully and to accept their words calmly and appreciatively. Then we can pray and reflect on what they said and decide on a course of action.

Since these accountability partners fulfill such an important role in our success as leaders, we need to choose them carefully, making it a matter of prayer and consideration. Most SWWs don't want their husbands to be their accountability partners (it's too hard for them to be objective), and they certainly don't want to encourage that kind of input from unsolicited volunteers or casual observers (we tend to get defensive and resent criticism from strangers or even friends who don't really know us).

My accountability partners are my younger sister and two of my best friends. Sometimes I'm tempted to resist if they point out something that needs attention, but then I remember that I'm the one who gave firm instructions about their duties. When one of these three women pulls me aside to talk to me about something, I do my best to let down my guard—open my heart, my mind, and my will—and humbly listen.

There's a saying, "It's hard to see the picture when you're sitting inside the frame." Ask your godly accountability partners to watch you from outside the frame as you serve, lead, and live all out for God.

THE BEAUTY OF DIVERSITY

I have many friends and colleagues who are women with strong will, intelligence, education, passion, purpose, and motivation. But each of them has different interests, and they've developed skills and talents in diverse fields and life paths. Many are more analytic and linear, drawn to math and science. They love figuring out a problem, designing a solution, and coming up with the right answer. Others, like me, are definitely big-picture thinkers. Rarely does their thinking go in a straight line. These people are generally drawn to the arts and humanities. They love collaboration as well as projects and problems with many solutions. If someone insists that we work in a particular leadership position, some of us will decline simply because the job doesn't fit.

Many of us may feel comfortable leading wherever God places us—whether it's in a traditional role or in a role occupied mostly by men. But just because our population is approximately 50 percent men and 50 percent women doesn't mean every man wants to be treated the same as a woman—or that every woman wants to be treated the same as a man.

Most SWWs don't want to get leadership roles just because it fulfills a quota for hiring a certain percentage of females. We don't succeed because we demand special consideration; we succeed because we demonstrate our ability to do the best job.

When I worked as a fully commissioned reserve police officer more than twenty-five years ago, my badge read "Patrolman." In the beginning I was the only female officer. I wore uniforms and Kevlar vests designed for men. My locker room was the tiny, one-person women's bathroom. I didn't care. I was just thrilled to be there, to have an opportunity to do what I felt passionately in my heart I was meant to do at that time in my life. I endured a lot of teasing and skepticism from my male counterparts during my first year on the streets. I didn't go in expecting my fellow officers to cut me any slack, yet I found that most of them were willing to help me as I worked hard to earn and maintain mutual respect.

By the second year, I was promoted to reserve director and began leading the department's twelve reserve officers. I served in that position for four years. Although I understood and participated in the core brotherhood component of law enforcement, I never tried to be just one of the guys. I worked hard to keep proving they could trust me to do the job and to have their backs in a dangerous and often hostile environment.

My aim was not to be the best *female* police officer; my goal was to be an outstanding police officer. Period. Diversity didn't mean making sure there were a certain number of women; it meant we appreciated the skills and dedication of everyone who was qualified to do the job.

In *Gifted to Lead,* Nancy Beach describes how she handled her leadership as programming director for many years at Willow Creek Community Church:

> I never want the fact that I am a woman to be the focal point of my work, and ideally, any other leaders I work with won't consider it a big deal either. My gender is really not the point. Actions speak much louder than words, so I want to focus on doing the work as best I can. Ultimately, this earns respect. If the issue of gender comes up at all, I want it to be more of an afterthought, as in, "Oh, by the way, our programming director [or teaching director] is a woman."[4]

That should always be our goal: to pursue leadership where we feel God has gifted and called us. If it's in a nontraditional role, then we must do it to the best of our ability, not to prove that a woman can do something just as well as a man, but to show that Christ has gifted us to do a job well and because we are qualified and called to do it.

True leadership is not confined to gender. *Harvard Business Review* blogger Tony Schwartz makes a compelling case for appreciating good leaders by recognizing how much we need men *and* women.

> An effective modern leader requires a blend of intellectual qualities—the ability to think analytically, strategically and creatively—and emotional ones, including self-awareness, empathy, and humility. In short, great leadership begins with being a whole human being.[5]

If your right hand reaches down to lift something heavy and it proves to be too much, does your left hand look down and say to the right hand, "Well, you shouldn't have even tried it. You know you can't do that by yourself," and let you go on struggling? No! Without a moment's hesitation, your left hand quickly swoops down and helps you lift the weight.

As members of the body of Christ, shouldn't such an automatic response be the natural one for us too? If we have to stop and debate the gender issue and whether we should help others or not—particularly those we are leading—are we living all out for God and representing Christ and His church? When we focus on and encourage individual strengths, we help build the body of Christ by identifying and appreciating how much we need one another—regardless of gender. This is a team effort.

Remember, if we spend our energies demanding to be

noticed and given preference simply because we're women, we might miss the success that comes as a result of demonstrating our capabilities and working shoulder to shoulder with women *and* men in the kingdom. That is the beauty of diversity.

LEADING FROM WHERE YOU ARE

Strong-willed women have a great variety of both callings and gifts, and their influence is needed in every area of service—paid or unpaid. We must never look at a leadership opportunity as too small or insignificant for us to make a difference. While many have leadership positions in professional fields, others exert their influence beautifully in leadership positions as unpaid volunteers. My friend Jean Daly is one of them. She explained to me why leading in volunteer positions is just as important and valuable to God's work:

> At this stage of my life, I organize many different things—foster-agency Christmas gift drives and events, football-award banquets, Bible studies, prayer meetings, school parties, and end-of-school banquets. I may not be a CEO, but I too strive to rally others to catch my vision. I respect their gifts and ideas, I delegate, and I try to lead with integrity.

Leadership opportunities are all around us. When you're a woman of strength and purpose, God has gifted you with some pretty amazing qualities, and He wants you to use those powerful gifts for His glory.

You're Never Leading Alone

Whether we lead a large corporation, an international ministry, or our own flock of future world changers, at some point even the strongest SWW realizes it's impossible to do everything on our own. We are, after all, mere mortals—and that's where we can call on our supernatural powers granted through the greatest Leader of all: Jesus Christ.

In *Leading and Loving It,* Lori Wilhite and Brandi Wilson give us a vivid picture to illustrate how this leadership ideal works:

> Have you ever been in one of those pedal boats out on the lake? You quickly spin your feet, kind of like Fred Flintstone and Barney Rubble in their foot-powered car. Your feet move, but somehow that boat barely budges. The waves push against you, and your kid in the passenger seat is no help whatsoever. You need a motor, an outside force, to propel you forward. Like everything else

in our lives and leadership, serving must be done through the power and strength of Jesus Christ.[6]

Did you catch that? The measure of a true leader isn't just how well she leads—it's how clearly and consistently she depends upon and lifts up Christ . . . and makes sure she's letting *Him* lead. What an incredible privilege it is to work for God!

PROFILES IN
Perseverance

CINDY BREILH

Cindy Breilh was driven to succeed from the very beginning. Whether it was sports, academics, or personal relationships, she pushed herself to become the top achiever. As a leader in high school, she found herself challenging the status quo whenever and wherever she could.

As the firstborn child of missionary parents serving in Ethiopia, Cindy grew up in a very fundamentalist, legalistic church. "As a child I was taught that women were essentially second-class citizens in many respects, and that there were certain things they could and could not do," she explains. But it was her strong will that caused her eventually to push back and question whether or not that was really the truth.

As Cindy became more and more rebellious against her fundamentalist upbringing, she also became increasingly frustrated with what she perceived to be hypocrisy and a lack of authentic faith in the church. When her parents and home church members objected to her interest in going to Bible school for a year before entering a university, she decided it was time to figure some things out for herself.

As she read her Bible, Revelation 3:15–16 leaped out at her: "I know your deeds, that you are neither cold nor hot. I wish you were either one or the other! So, because you are lukewarm—neither hot nor cold—I am about to spit you out of my mouth" (NIV). Cindy made up her mind that when it came to believing and serving God, she was going to study the Bible for a year and then make a decision to be hot or cold. Being lukewarm at *anything* was simply *not* an option for her.

Her yearlong journey at Bible school resulted in an all-or-nothing decision to be *hot,* and her commitment to follow Jesus took her to a university where she could study medicine. She began to sense that God was calling her to prepare herself to serve overseas when she saw international students living out their faith in so many ways that were different from her narrow Western evangelical perspective. As she watched these other believers, she thought, *You mean you can worship God that way and He hears you?*

"I was realizing that God's people are praying all over the world and He hears them in multiple languages and in multiple ways—why do we think there's only one narrow way to serve Him?"

She had a natural bent toward the medical profession, but her father convinced her that she should not be a doctor. So she enrolled in nursing school and, of course, excelled in her field. As she worked as a top-level nurse, she again realized how important the influence of strong-willed women could be and decided again to rebel—this time against the hierarchy of medicine, which she had determined was discriminatory against women.

This led Cindy to step out of clinical nursing, go to business school, and start her own business. She realized that one of the biggest obstacles for women in medicine was not just having to juggle multiple responsibilities; it was also the overall culture of nursing school and the dominant male bias that was often demeaning to women. But what if prospective nurses could enroll in classes they could complete in their own homes? This was in the early '80s, before there was such a thing as video rentals or Internet learning, but Cindy had a dream, and she wasn't about to do anything but accept the challenge of figuring out how to make it come true.

Cindy worked hard to make her new business a success, which then launched her into the world of marketing and program development. She even served on several nonprofit boards. The seed in her heart that had been planted through the international students at her university blossomed into a vision of spreading the message of encouragement and empowerment for women around the world. Soon she started working for Agros International, a nongovernmental organization (NGO) in Central America, and she turned her passion into purpose, helping families develop skills for working themselves out of poverty. Through Agros she discovered the powerful difference it made when they were able to strengthen women in these poverty-stricken communities and bring them into equal partnership with men in order to help the whole community thrive.

When she talks about her experience at Agros, Cindy leans forward and gets an intense look on her face. She's convinced that we can go into any community that's not thriving, look at the position and status of women and their opportunities, and see a direction correlation between that and poverty, poor health, and lack of resources. She's passionate about reaching women around the world and improving the whole community by valuing and lifting their status and importance to the family.

"We need to tell this story," Cindy insists. "Not only do we need to do it in the developing world, but we also need to bring it to our own country and empower and embolden women here, because I believe the same thing is true. As women come into equal partnership with men, communities thrive, peace breaks out, and children are cared for."

When World Vision offered Cindy the position of national director of Women of Vision, Cindy's professional expertise was deepened by her personal experience as a wife and mother of three. She was energized by the challenge of finding ways women all over the world could balance the responsibilities of the home with the incredible privilege of working for the kingdom of God. She brought her conviction that one of the biggest tensions we have as women of faith is that there are competing theologies and people who simply want to say a woman's place is in the home, or in the kitchen, or just raising children. But some of us have energy that we want to give back. All during that time we still want children, we still want to work, we still want good marriages, and we want to be able to combine all those things.

"If you take a good look," Cindy points out, "even homeschool moms or homemakers, especially if they are strong-willed women, are the ones organizing the co-op group, or heading up a committee, or doing all kinds of tasks. You never just sit at home and do nothing. And really, if you look at it globally, there are no women who are *only* homemakers."

If you ask Cindy if she would call herself a "feminist," she'll shake her head and tell you she's all about "gender equity"—and it's not the same as the popular definition of feminism. She'll tell you that feminism is focused primarily on empowering women, which says, "Women, you are strong—let's hear you roar." But Cindy believes gender equity speaks more to the fact that we include men *and* women in this journey. It's not just about empowering women; it's also bringing men alongside to understand women and the power and purpose of women in relationship and in the world.

She's convinced that gender equity is biblical. We are equal partners, co-creators, and part of God's redemptive work in this world. "I've been discouraged at times by those who say, 'This is the only way you can be a woman,'" she says. "Everything about how God created me—my genetic makeup, my environment, my passion—everything screams that can't be true."

After several years with Women of Vision, Cindy is, at this writing, the director of advancement for

Medical Teams International (MTI), an organization that provides medical and dental care, humanitarian aid, and development programs to people around the world. The president of MTI says this about Cindy: "She is a person of deep faith, with extraordinary capability and relationship-building talent and an abiding passion for coming alongside the most marginalized people in the world."

Cindy doesn't show any signs of slowing down as she leads the way in strengthening and empowering women to become equal partners with men in efforts to alleviate poverty all over the world. She has seen the difference it can make, and she remains undaunted in her mission.

STRONG-WILLED WOMEN AND THE MEN WHO *Love* THEM

'd like to clear up one thing right away: I'm not a marriage expert, nor do I play one on TV. This chapter won't give you advice based on clinical research. This is a chapter filled with strong-willed women speaking from experience—sharing struggles and giving insight into what we've discovered about why and how marriage relationships are so challenging when an SWW is involved.

Most SWWs handle marriage the way we do almost everything else—we have the capacity to bring out both great passion and great friction. We're rarely indifferent, and we don't usually suffer silently. There are exceptions, but in general our husbands receive clear opinions and reactions from us most of the time, whether they like it or not. Since we bring strength and purpose to other areas of our lives, it makes sense that God can use them in our marriages as well.

How Can Being an SWW Strengthen Your Marriage?

Strong-willed women can quickly identify some obvious advantages we bring to a marriage. On my survey, when I asked SWWs what their husbands liked best about their strong-willed nature, the participants shared similar answers. The most popular answers had to do with how fiercely loyal we are when it comes to commitment and dedication, and how we don't quit just because things get difficult or inconvenient.

When it comes to marriage, we know how valuable our strengths can be as part of a team—when we're willing to work as one. One SWW wrote: "My husband says that we seem to balance each other out. There are areas where I'm strong and he's not, as well as areas where he's strong and I'm not. Sometimes it requires considerable conviction and commitment when, as a couple, we face a lot of challenges and pressure."

That's true, especially, when we're faced with handling those difficult issues alone—such as for an SWW who is in the military or married to someone who is. One SWW military wife said, "When my husband is on military deployments he knows that I can handle myself and protect our house and family. He doesn't worry about me falling to pieces." Another SWW, Cathy, sums it up well when she says, "My determination not to give up gives my husband confidence."

There's no doubt about the importance of keeping our strengths firmly in line with our desire to bring honor and glory to God. We're committed, loyal, and we'll fight for our marriage. Those are good strengths to possess. However, as we know too well, the desire for a great marriage that honors God doesn't always translate easily into day-to-day reality. In fact, there are a few areas in marriage that pose universal challenges for SWWs. Before we talk about some of those, though, let's take a quick look at the men we married.

THE MEN WHO LOVE STRONG-WILLED WOMEN

When my city's local Christian radio station helped me host the first "Strong-Willed Women and the Men Who Love Them" conference a few years ago, I wasn't sure what to expect. It was well attended by married couples, along with a few singles mixed in. There were two overarching rules for the weekend: (1) Love the Lord your God with all your heart, and (2) Love your neighbor as yourself (based on the passage from Matthew

22:37–39). That means, we explained, that everything we say and do is intended to honor God, and also that we do not criticize or complain about our neighbor (or, in this case, our spouse). It wasn't a traditional marriage seminar; it was a weekend dedicated to learning about and understanding how being an SWW affects the deepest and most sacred relationship next to the one we have with God.

It wasn't hard to imagine what the energy level would be when almost a hundred SWWs were in the same room—but what about the men who loved them? What would they be like? Was there a stereotype that would emerge? Is there a particular type of man who is naturally drawn to an SWW?

We quickly discovered the answer: No. In fact, if the husbands at the conference were any indication, the men who love strong-willed women are as complex and diverse as SWWs themselves. Some husbands were quiet; some were outgoing; many were analytic and methodical; others were intuitive and creative. It was impossible to fit them into any one or two categories, which just proved again that we can't assume that all men or all women are alike—sometimes temperament, style, and personality trump gender. Our conference was a great example of the diversity in the men who loved their SWWs.

When we had a session that divided men and women into separate rooms, I was surprised at how quickly the men warmed up to the idea of talking to one another about their strong-willed wives. This was one of those rare, socially acceptable opportunities to compare notes with other husbands of SWWs and find out what they had in common. The guidelines were clear—no complaining, criticizing, or faultfinding on the part of husbands *or* wives. But the conversation was fascinating and enlightening.

I have to admit I hadn't expected the response from such a variety of men who had all agreed to come to a weekend relationship seminar with their strong-willed wives (although we *did* hold it at a hot springs resort). They were animated, engaged, and positive when they talked about their wives, and they were encouraging and upbeat when they reassured one another that the challenges they faced were not unique. Many times the room was filled with laughter amid the many nodding heads, and when the time for discussion was up, they didn't want to leave. They wanted to discover and share more secrets for success when it comes to being married to an SWW.

As the conference participants quickly discovered, there are many issues common to every marriage, but there are a few that pose special challenges for the SWW and her spouse.

WHO'S IN CHARGE?

Ed was about to walk out the door when his wife, Lisa, asked him, "Is that what you're going to wear today?" Ed paused and gave her a crooked smile. "Apparently not," he replied and headed back to his bedroom closet to try again. He's learned to trust his wife on matters of style when it comes to clothes. And yet Lisa trusts Ed with other important matters.

The same is true in my marriage. My husband, Jack, trusts me on many issues, and I trust him on others. For instance, when I'm writing a book or article, I almost always ask Jack to read it before I submit it. I need his analytical and objective opinion, even though I sometimes bristle at his critique. But I've learned to trust his judgment and benefit from his input.

When we trust and listen to each other in marriage, we use complementary strengths, which means neither spouse is the boss. Over the years many SWWs have discovered which spouse steps up in different situations, based on strengths, not competing for who gets to be in charge. Every good marriage has give-and-take, along with a strong trust in our spouse. For the SWW whose desire is to live all out for God, there's something even more important in her practical understanding of marriage: to have a successful marriage, she needs to have the foundation of a solid-rock faith in Christ, and an unshakeable commitment to both the man she married and the God she serves.

One of the foundational Bible passages for marriage is Ephesians 5:21–28. Here it is, with my comments in brackets:

Out of respect for Christ, be courteously reverent to one another. Wives, understand and support your husbands in ways that show your support for Christ. [*That makes sense.*]

The husband provides leadership to his wife the way Christ does to his church, not by domineering but by cherishing. [*Cherishing, yes, that sounds great—I want to be cherished.*]

So just as the church submits to Christ as he exercises such leadership, wives should likewise submit to their husbands. [*Wait a minute. I'm fine with submitting to Christ, but my husband? What if he takes advantage of that?*]

Husbands, go all out in your love for your wives, exactly as Christ did for the church—a love marked by giving, not getting. Christ's love makes the church whole. . . . Everything he does and says is designed to bring the best out of her. . . . And that is how husbands ought to love their wives. They're really doing themselves a favor—since they're already "one" in marriage. [*That sounds like good teamwork to me.*]

Every SWW has to wrestle with the concept of submission—not just to God, but also a biblical submission to her husband's leadership in marriage. No SWW wants to be a doormat, and no husband of an SWW wants to be continually overruled in his leadership. The foundation of our commitment to God is trust—total and complete trust in Him. This same trust needs to be in place with our husband in order for the covenant of our marriage to thrive.

If we want our marriage to bring honor and glory to God, we must consciously keep Christ at the center of it. He is Lord of our lives; He is in control, and we trust Him as we submit to our husband out of love and honor for God.

But what does that mean on a practical level? Certainly under this biblical framework, men cannot justify domination or abuse in the name of submission. Neither can women justify emasculating their husbands in an effort to be in charge. Marriage works best when we honor each other and both of us honor God.

Kay describes what worked in her struggle: "Deciding to put others first has helped me channel my will in a direction that respects and loves my husband rather than trying to control him."

Okay, you might be thinking, *but shouldn't he do the same for me?* Yes. But even if he doesn't, we trust God to help us work through the conflict without destroying the relationship with either our husband *or* God.

Remember, I'm not a marriage expert, and even the best

marriages will sometimes have serious issues to work out. There are great resources available to help address those issues. But for our purposes here, let's look at two or three practical and immediately useful ways that we, as SWWs, can appreciate the men we married, reduce the natural tendency for tension and conflict, and maybe even make our marriages more fun.

How Much Conflict Is Normal?

"Do you think everyone has as much conflict as we do?"

My husband's question caught me by surprise. "We don't have *that* much conflict," I protested.

He nodded vigorously. "Yes. We *do*. See? We're even arguing about not having conflict."

"This isn't arguing," I objected. "It's discussion, normal conversational discourse."

He shook his head. "Normal for *you,* maybe, but not for me."

Jack likes things to go smoothly and predictably. He has boxes and categories and expectations. He analyzes, processes, and moves at his own pace. But I have no boxes; I'm more spontaneous and intuitive, and I definitely want everyone else to move at *my* pace. This isn't just a gender issue—some men are more like me, and many women are more like Jack. But the point is, when two people who are so different from each other get married, there's bound to be conflict—that's a normal part of living together. But when you factor in the trait of being an SWW, the definition of *normal* shifts significantly. Many SWWs learn best when we argue, preferring to wrestle with issues by way of verbal fencing—iron sharpening iron.[1]

In their book *The Good Fight,* Doctors Les and Leslie Parrott share research that shows the average married couple argues about small things as much as 312 times per year. "That means most couples experience a tug-of-war of some kind on a near-daily basis," they write.[2] Even these two marriage experts freely confess to having their fair share of squabbles.

A lot of us marry a man who's drastically different from us because at first it seems like a refreshing perspective. We're drawn to opposites because we sense the need for complementary strengths, and because we admire a man who has the abilities we lack. But on a day-to-day basis, no matter how much we love him, it turns out not to be that refreshing. After all, we're living proof that *our* way works—and it's often hard to convince an SWW that she shouldn't use her way!

It's like the design of our body. God designed us to have a right hand and a left hand. We wouldn't get much done if we used two right hands or two left hands—we need one of each, with a very different perspective and approach. Suppose the right hand *did* convince the left hand to be the same as the right? Very quickly we'd discover that we can't accomplish much at all. We're unique for a reason, but we need each other's strengths to be a good team. And when we stop to think about it, we usually admit we admired our husbands for some of the very things that now may drive us crazy.

Conflict in marriage is normal. But if you sense that your marriage has an abundance of conflict, it may be time to evaluate how much your strong will might have to do with it. To help you have less conflict and more cooperation, consider the following two suggestions.

Keep Your Sense of Humor

One of the things I love most about my husband, Jack, is his lack of guile. He says what he means, and sometimes he says the wrong thing, but he never has a hidden agenda, nor does he use subtle manipulation. He told me before we got married that there would be times when I would need to take his face in my hands, look him straight in the eyes, and say, "Jack, this is what I need." Here's one of my favorite examples of a time when I had to employ that strategy.

We were taking ballroom dancing lessons in order to learn to waltz. At one point, the instructor told us to hold on to each other but leave a little more room between us. As she walked away, Jack said quietly, "Well, we don't need to leave more room, because we're big and wide."

I looked incredulously at him. "Big and wide?"

"Sure," he replied. "Look at her." He was pointing to the cute petite instructor.

Thinking maybe he hadn't seen my shocked and hurt reaction the first time, I repeated his words: *Big and wide?"*

He shrugged. "Okay," he said, "big and tall, then."

As I took his face in my hands, I saw his expression change. "Jack," I said calmly, "stop talking."

He nodded and quickly agreed. "Yeah, I think that would be a good idea."

We both laughed, and that was the end of an argument that never actually began—and the birth of a great illustration for my seminars!

One of the best ways to keep your sense of humor when your husband is driving you crazy is to remember that he doesn't usually annoy you on purpose. It might *seem* like that sometimes, but the two of you see the world from very different perspectives, and you're typically doing things the way that makes sense to you. We can't always remember this in the heat of the moment, but with practice, we can reduce the number of times we jump straight into an argument before we stop to consider that he may just be doing what comes naturally.

Sometimes Jack and I will agree ahead of time to do things from the other person's perspective. "Let me just be analytical for a few minutes, okay?" he'll say. Or I'll state, "I need to give you a big picture, and then I'll get to the details, all right?" During a conversation I can stop him and ask something like, "It's a bit theoretical for me. Can you give me a quick summary first?"

Awareness is half the battle, and if we can recognize *why* the other person is irritating us and then lighten up in our response, there may be at least a few arguments where we can substitute a smile and a shake of the head for the angry words we were about to say.

Ask More Questions and Issue Fewer Statements

Early in our marriage I told Jack, "If you can ask me a question instead of telling me what to do, it almost always improves my cooperation level." Then I gave him some examples, such as instead of saying, "I can't believe you just did that," try, "Is that what you meant to do?" Or instead of saying, "Don't miss that left turn," try, "Do you want to turn left here?"

I know—as you read this you may think, *I can see right through that approach; I know he's saying things that way just to get me to cooperate with him.* Well, what's wrong with that? When Jack uses questions this way, it's true that I quickly recognize what he's doing, but I'm happy that he's making the effort. It means he's going out of his way to say something in a way that helps me understand and accept it. It's not as if he's pulling one over on me or anything—he and I both know it's a deliberate approach. But it isn't just how my husband needs to respond; it's how I need to respond too. Instead of throwing out a demand at him, he cooperates better with me when I offer him that same respect. I don't know about you, but even if it reduces the small yearly conflicts to fewer than three hundred, I'm all in favor of it.

WHAT MAKES IT WORTH THE EFFORT?

One of the most encouraging sentences the Parrotts offer in *The Good Fight* is this one: "Couples who stay happily married disagree just as much as couples who get divorced, but they have learned how to use those disagreements to deepen their connection."[3]

It may take some time, some trial and error, and maybe even some counseling, but no one is better equipped to stay committed to our marriages for the long run than SWWs. We don't just quit. We hate to give up. We can pretty much do anything we set our minds to do. That means we can love more deeply, serve more humbly, and give more honestly.

The best part of all? We serve the Overcomer, and when we stay close to Christ, He fills in the gaps of our wisdom with grace and understanding. You just can't get better than that!

MOMS AND KIDS WHO *Share* STRONG WILL

Three-year-old Emily was not having a good day. Sarah, her SWW mom, wasn't having a good day, either. This morning's conflict was a full-on battle of strong wills. Emily preferred the bright yellow pants over her mother's choice of beige, and they were already going to be late for preschool. There had been screaming—on both the mother's and daughter's parts—and now Sarah was putting her foot down. She pulled the beige pants on her daughter, over Emily's wild and vocal protests, dragged her out to the car, then buckled her into her car seat. It had taken almost superhuman strength and a will of steel, but Sarah had won. Exhausted, she started the car and pulled out into traffic. Suddenly Emily fell silent. Sarah gave a sigh of relief. Then, moments later, Emily's voice came quietly but triumphantly from the backseat. "I just peed my pants."

Life with a strong-willed child (SWC) is unlike any other experience you'll ever have. If you have any doubts about that, check with your parents. Although it doesn't always feel like it, God paid you a great compliment when He entrusted you with this bundle of raw strength and will. He's given you the responsibility to teach, guide, and nurture this life that will change the world—one way or the other.

The good news is that as an SWW, you're in a much better position than most to understand how your SWC's mind works, and you can anticipate and prevent some of the mistakes your own parents may have made with you. The bad news is that in many ways, because you both have strong wills, parenting can be more difficult when your child decides to stand toe-to-toe with you and neither of you wants to back down. So just in case you could use a quick refresher course on how to deal with an SWC, I've put some ideas in this chapter.

Over the past thirty years, I've worked with hundreds of strong-willed children and adults of all ages and from all walks of life. It's still surprising to see how much they all agree on certain basics when it comes to what brings out the best in a strong-willed person of virtually *any* age. Here are three critical elements for success.

CRITICAL ELEMENT 1: CREATE AND CULTIVATE A RELATIONSHIP WITH YOUR SWC THAT HE OR SHE WANTS TO PRESERVE

I was giving a parenting seminar for women police officers when one frustrated mom said, "I'm very good at being a cop, but my sixteen-year-old strong-willed daughter drives me crazy. When I went to pick her up at her dad's, she told me she wasn't going to go home with me and I couldn't make her. After a big argument, I finally put her in a suspect come-along hold and put her in the car." We all gasped, and she said, "I *know*—but I didn't know what else to do!"

The SWC, regardless of age, has a natural resistance to positional authority. That's the kind of authority you find in the military or in law enforcement—where you're required to obey purely because the person who issues the orders is your superior officer. It doesn't matter how you feel about that person—your job is to obey. Period. But parenting doesn't work very well if that's your only approach.

As an SWW, you already know that no SWC likes being around someone who's always issuing commands. There needs to be an *up*side to the parent-child connection instead of just an overwhelming amount of demands and correction. If your SWC feels valued and understood, there's a better chance that your child will work to preserve that relationship by cooperating with and obeying you.

When my SWC, Mike, was fourteen, I had to take an out-of-town trip. Because I was a single parent at the time, I asked my good friend Autumn to chaperone Mike and his brother, Rob, at home. While I was away, I received a call from Mike.

"Mom, I'm going with my friends to a movie tonight, okay?"

I asked which movie they were planning to see and he told me. *The Omen.* "Mike, you know you're not allowed to see R-rated movies. You need to make a different choice."

Although exasperated, he agreed. Then he said, "Oh, and I want to go over to Michelle's house afterward with my friends."

I kept my voice calm. "Mike, you know that when I'm out of town, I don't want you to go over to Michelle's house. Just hang out with your friends for a while at the sandwich shop next to the theater, and Autumn will pick you up there and take you home."

He sighed loudly. "Fine."

Later that night I called home and talked to Autumn. "Well, Mike went to the right movie," she said. Then she added, "But he called and had me pick him up at Michelle's house." I frowned and started to protest, but she continued, "I know he wasn't supposed to, and I told him he was going to be in a lot of trouble for disobeying you. He just said, 'I don't care what she does to me. I had fun and it was worth it.'"

Whoa! I told her I'd deal with him when I got home.

When I got home, I said to Mike, "Thanks for going to the right movie." He nodded. "And I heard you went to Michelle's house, even though I specifically told you not to do that."

He stuck his chin up in the air as he replied, "Well, I had a lot of fun, and it was worth whatever you do to punish me."

It was my turn to nod, but then I looked him directly in the eyes. "Mike, you know you're dealing with the queen of strong will, right?" He shrugged, and I continued. "In my whole life there's always been one punishment that wasn't worth it."

He grudgingly asked, "What?"

"Losing a relationship that's really important to me."

He knew I was referring to the close bond he and I had, and he immediately dropped his head and said, "I'm sorry, Mom."

Now that wouldn't have worked if I hadn't already spent years building a solid and positive relationship through some very difficult times with my strong-willed son. But I knew that keeping our relationship strong really mattered to him.

"So what's my punishment?" he asked in a resigned tone. I couldn't resist using an effective technique I learned from a book titled *Parenting with Love and Logic*.[1] "Well, Mike, I want to sleep on it—think and pray about it, and I'll let you know in the morning." He hated the suspense. He just wanted to get the whole thing over with right away. He knew that waiting was part of the punishment itself.

The next morning I assigned him ten hours of volunteer work with the senior citizens at our church, and he did it without complaint.

The relationship you nurture won't be the same for every SWC. Part of what makes the connection so special is your recognition and appreciation of how your child is unique.

In the heat of the battle, if you have the kind of relationship that your child wants to preserve, you have leverage. Then, even if you occasionally lose your cool or make a parenting mistake, your SWC will still work on making sure your bond stays solid.

The bonus here is that you don't have to be the best parent in the neighborhood; you don't have to be the most creative, energetic, or intelligent adult in your child's life. If you work at keeping a healthy relationship, your child will always have a great reason to obey you and follow your guidance.

CRITICAL ELEMENT 2: REMAIN CALM, FIRM, AND RESPECTFUL

She was a beautiful little girl, probably about four or five, and she was sitting in her mother's cart at Target, lovingly holding a package containing a Barbie doll. Mom was looking at office supplies, and the little girl was loudly complaining: "Mom, I'm bored! I said I'm bored! I am really, *really* bored!"

Her mother looked at her calmly and said, "If you tell me you're bored again, we are simply going to leave right now and go straight home."

The little girl looked slyly at her mother as she smugly said, "We won't leave without paying for this stuff."

Her mother didn't miss a beat. Without even raising her voice, she replied quietly, "But we *will* be leaving without Barbie." Her daughter immediately fell silent. Hooray for Mom. She got authority and respect, and neither one of them had a temper tantrum.

Remember, you're modeling the behavior and tone of voice you want your SWC to use. If you lose your temper or raise your voice in anger, your child may either match your tone and stance, or shut down altogether. Heather, an SWW who claims *all* her children are strong-willed, recalls her own childhood years to help her remember how important it is not to let her children make her angry: "When I discipline, I do it dispassionately (what I mean is that I remain calm, especially when they're not, and allow them time and space to think it through before we talk about it). I remember feeling in control when my silence would make my mom so angry—I felt like I was winning. This is why I keep my anger out of it."

There will be times when you lose your composure or you're so frustrated that you simply can't keep your temper in check. Then something happens we call the "we can dish it out but we can't take it" syndrome. The moment you hear yourself say angry words, you know your SWC is probably not going to do what you said—after all, you wouldn't do it either if the roles were reversed. ("You're going to stop crying right now, or I'm going to give all your toys away!") But you're the parent, and as an SWW, you inherently have no reverse gear. So what do you do?

If you can pull yourself back together, stop and ask for a do-over. Make it clear that even though you're not apologizing for *what* you asked, you're sorry for the *way* you asked. Then say, "Let's start over, okay?"

One survey participant, Diane, remembers learning some lessons the hard way with her SWC. "It's worth backing down sometimes. Not every fight needs to be fought. There are so many molehills I made into mountains because things had to be done my way. Letting your child know that you are not only listening but that you also *hear* her makes a big difference."

If you can't bring yourself to ask for a calmer do-over at that moment, take a break and put some space between the two of you—then start again after both of you gain composure.

CRITICAL ELEMENT 3: MAKE SURE YOUR SWC
KNOWS YOUR LOVE IS UNCONDITIONAL

When you tell your SWC, "I'll love you no matter what," don't be surprised if you get tested on whether or not that's really true. *How about this? Will you love me now? What about this?*

And sometimes SWCs, based on your reactions, believe you don't *really* love them no matter what—you love them only if they do what you say, or if they follow your rules.

SWCs understand there are consequences to their choices; they understand they can't get by with bad behavior. But if the ultimate consequence is having you withdraw your love, how can they count on ever being loved unconditionally by God? This is where it gets difficult. This is where it will take all the strength and love you have in order to deal with the situations and circumstances that will arise.

Dena is an SWW with six kids, most of whom are strong-willed. She says she recommends that all strong-willed moms do what she does every day, which not only helps her children but also keeps her sane:

Pray, pray, pray. Cover your children in prayer. Become
a prayer warrior for yourself and them. Pray God's
Word over them. Be ready to choose battles carefully

and show mercy. We are a reflection of Christ to our children. They need to look at us and see Him. There should be no question of whether you love them or not. Just as there is no question of God's unfailing, unconditional love for us, and *that* incredible unconditional love draws us to Him. *That* is what I want my child to know. I love my child, period. There are no conditions she must meet. I simply love her. And that will never change.

Try to think about how much God trusted you when He gave you this SWC. You can't give up just because the going gets tough or you don't feel up to the job. There's no place you can go to officially resign. You can do this.

In case you start feeling like a failure, remember this: God Himself is the perfect parent—yet He still has wayward children. He does not force them to serve Him. He does not run roughshod over their free will. Yes, there are certain immutable laws of the universe, certain inevitable consequences for disobedience, but He never stops loving them, even when they don't love Him back. He accepts them as they are, opens His arms when they weep, and keeps the table set for their return.

In *Bringing Home the Prodigals,* Rob Parsons wrote a story that exemplifies this kind of unconditional love for a child.

Shortly after one of the Bringing Home the Prodigals events, a woman wrote to me. She told me that her daughter had walked out of their home when she was eighteen years old. She had turned her back not only on her mother and father, but on the God she had once loved. "My daughter didn't get in touch, and we didn't know whether she was alive or dead," the woman wrote. She went on to tell me that every night, as she and her husband turned off the lights before they went to bed, she would always say to him, "Leave the porch light on." And every Christmas, she would put a little Christmas tree in the front of the house, its lights shining, just as she used to when her daughter was at home.

After six years, her daughter suddenly came home—and not just to her mother and father, but to God. When she did, she told her mother a remarkable story: "Mom, I so often wanted to come home, but I was too ashamed. Sometimes, in the early hours of the morning, I would drive my car onto your street and just sit there. I used to gaze at the houses and every one of them was dark apart from our house: you always left a light on. And at Christmas I would do the same: just sit there in the darkness and look at the Christmas tree you had put outside—I knew it was for me."[2]

I've had so many moms tell me they wish they could have known about how to handle an SWC twenty-five or thirty years ago. Now their child is an adult, grown and gone, and there doesn't seem to be any chance for reconciliation. Here's what I know: as long as you and your SWC are both alive, it's not too late. Never give up. Never stop praying. Never stop reaching out in love, even if your child ignores you. If you're an SWW, you know that it's common practice when you rebel not to let those who love you know they're getting through to you, even when they are.

It Will Be Worth It

I first wrote *You Can't Make Me! (But I Can Be Persuaded)* when my own SWC, Mike, was still very young. I was in the trenches as a mom and teacher, and I wanted to share insights and strategies for bringing out the best in a strong-willed child. Many years later, I wrote a new version of the book, updating and adding new material—including a lot of what I had used with Mike as he grew up.

Mike was home for the summer before his junior year of college, and he was working as a counselor at a YMCA camp. On one of his days off, he came for a visit and plopped down in a chair in our living room.

"Mom," he said, "some of those kids are driving me so crazy, I decided it was time I read your book about strong-willed children."

I raised my eyebrows and asked a question I wasn't sure I wanted to hear an answer to. "What did you think?"

He leaned forward in his chair and looked me in the eye. "It works!" Then he spent the next twenty minutes quoting passages from my book and interjecting several times with phrases like "And I really like using this one" or "This one works every time!"

I was stunned by his revelation and couldn't help putting something in the introduction of the revised edition of *You Can't Make Me!*:

By far the most meaningful endorsement I could ask for is the one from Mike. After twenty years of living with and loving my strong-willed child, after the prayers and tears, trial and error, perseverance and frustration, failure and success, he is reading and enjoying the book that describes him as the quintessential strong-willed kid. . . .

Believe me when I say I'm still in the trenches with you. I've parented a great strong-willed child and his equally wonderful but more compliant twin brother. I will never be able to make the claim I did everything right. Far from it! I am eternally grateful that God has been gracious in supplementing my well-intentioned and often inadequate efforts with His grace, love, and wisdom. . . .

Most of all, no matter how things turn out, I pray you will be glad you never gave up on the relationship with your strong-willed child. You'll never be able to truly measure what a difference it will make.[3]

I still stand by those words.

RITA HERNANDEZ

Rita Hernandez has a powerful love for God and country—actually, *two* countries. And Rita's vision has made a profound impact in both of them.

Rita was born in Mexico to a strong-willed mom who, against all odds, established the first bilingual school in Tijuana more than fifty years ago so that children living in this border town could have the benefit of mastering both Spanish and English. By the time she was eight years old, Rita had made up her mind to be a teacher, and since she had inherited her mother's strong will and an excellent bilingual education, nothing was going to get in her way.

She admits that she absorbed everything her mother taught her, and one of her strengths as a learner was that she was constantly on the lookout for new information and better ways of doing things. She worked hard and passed all the necessary tests to enter college at age fifteen, where she specialized in bilingual and bicultural education. Her main desire was to be the best teacher in the world. "I loved every moment," she says.

Rita came to the United States for the first time in

1985 when she was a senior in college, and she became a permanent resident in 1986 when she married. After teaching at both public and private schools for eleven years in the United States, Rita learned that her mom's school was suffering financially, so she returned to Tijuana with a mind full of knowledge and a strong desire to save her mom's school from financial disaster.

While she was there she determined to fulfill her vision to start a full English-language immersion program. So she would teach the children the history, government, language, and all cultural aspects of both countries. Her mom let her start with a preschool. "The results were beyond my imagination," she says with a smile. In two short years her preschool classes went from fifty-six students to a hundred and fifty. It was so successful that the parents of those children wanted to know why she and her mom didn't start an elementary school too.

So Rita, along with her husband, embarked on what Rita calls "the crazy adventure" of founding their own elementary school in which all grades up to sixth would include the English immersion program. They started with 120 students and 7 employees, and ten years later they had 352 students and 45 employees.

Soon, her sisters, also teachers, decided to follow Rita's vision, and their immersion program expanded to cover preschool through twelfth grade.

Rita had to overcome serious obstacles to see her vision fulfilled, but when you ask her about them, this resilient strong-willed woman (twelve on a scale of one to twelve) is quick to give God the glory and is humble enough to acknowledge her personal struggles along the journey.

> Nothing is impossible with God. The school is still standing after huge financial crises—our faith is still unshakeable. Even when we were running in the red, we still had faith. Seeing the school still standing today is a miracle. God has spoken to me often about His grace and understanding—what it is and how everything that He gained at the cross was for me (peace, power, understanding, healing, revelation). His love is amazing, and it changes my life on so many levels.

She admits that many of the obstacles she encountered were a direct result of her strong will sometimes going sideways. "It was hard to lower my expectations when it came to the pace of our progress," she admits.

"Not everybody can keep up with me. It's hard to choose people and then let go of what they do or don't do without feeling disappointed and let down." To help her continual desire for growth and maturity, she loves to be a student herself. "I still take classes," she says. The two areas of learning Rita identifies as having made the most difference for her? "Learning styles taught by Cynthia Tobias and the concept of boundaries as written about by John Townsend and Henry Cloud."

Another benefit she's received through the process of launching and running the school has been in her marriage. In the thirty years she and her husband have been married, they've experienced wonderful growth and closeness. "We've learned how to work together toward our goals," she says. And she's had to learn "how to go at his pace and not always expect him to run at mine. I'm very blessed that my husband has grown with me and that he is able to say, 'It's okay,' and, 'We can handle this together.'"

It won't surprise you to know that Rita still has an amazing vision for how God can use her talents and abilities to bridge the two countries she loves, especially when it comes to working with Hispanic women—and particularly those who are strong-willed, as she is. That's because in Mexico, she explains, "Hispanic strong-willed women are considered out of order and are not the status quo." Overall, Mexico has a very patriarchal culture, so according to Rita, a woman who makes more noise than her male counterpart is not received well.

She's enthusiastic about expanding her ministry. "I'm excited to share with other strong-willed Hispanic women the ways God can use them and help them fulfill their purpose and vision.

"I'm almost fifty years old," she continues, "and I've had to overcome many of those fears as I struggled with strong-willed parts of me. How could I work my strong will into the church culture?"

Because of Rita's great burden for young Hispanic women, God gave her a dream to start a new ministry fighting human trafficking in her hometown of Tijuana. A few years later the vision grew when she was invited to be mentored by one of the foremost authorities on human trafficking, Rosi Orozco, another strong-willed woman who is changing the world.

Through a step of faith, Rita and her husband moved to Mexico City, where Rita is now the executive director of Comisión Unidos Vs. Trata, an internationally renowned organization that fights human trafficking. At the writing of this book, Rita has turned the elementary school over to her sister so Rita can focus her energies on what some would call an impossible mission. But she is undaunted. "It's a huge job that only God knows how to do. For the first time in my life, I am totally dependent on Him. Many think I am crazy, but I believe that we can stop human trafficking in Mexico in my children's generation."

And I think she just might do it!

MENTORING
THE NEXT
Generation

Who do you and your peers hold up as good examples for how to be a godly, strong-willed woman?" I was having coffee with my younger friend Megan. She had just passed her twenty-seventh birthday, and she was working on a master's degree. She'd agreed to help me make sure this book was relevant to strong-willed women like her, and she'd already given me some good insights. This question, however, made her pause and think for a moment before she answered.

"You know, I don't think of any particular names when it comes to strong women we want to pattern our lives after," she confessed. "There are a lot of pretty cool women who are interesting and successful in the world today, but no names jump to mind that everyone my age would recognize and want to imitate. A lot of times if we aren't sure what to do, we just sort of have to compare notes with one another and figure it out."

I was saddened by that reality, but nodded my understanding. After all, the younger generations with their technology are more peer-oriented than ever. Instead of seeking information from experts or books, they've learned that the quickest way to find answers is to use their smartphone to check with friends or acquaintances and find out what they know or think. The importance and influence of a peer group is greater than it's ever been—but these voices don't always send the right messages, and in fact, sometimes they're downright inaccurate or confusing.

Megan told me she and most of her friends recently had read a life-changing book by Dr. Meg Jay called *The Defining Decade: Why Your Twenties Matter and How to Make the Most of Them Now.* She explained that she and many of her peers closely identify with Ian, one of Dr. Jay's clients who compared his twentysomething years to being in the middle of the ocean in totally unmarked waters. He felt so overwhelmed by the fact that he could swim anywhere that he just kept swimming in circles. He couldn't see land in any direction.

"That's what a lot of my friends feel like," said Megan. "We've been told we can do anything we really want to, achieve anything we set our minds to, and hold out for the perfect job that's out there somewhere. But then we're swept away by so many possibilities, we're almost paralyzed by the uncertainty of what direction to take. Since no one wants to make us feel like we're limited by anything, we don't really get any specific advice about what to do. We can't see any land."

She went on to say that she was personally mentoring a seventeen-year-old SWW because she believed it would have been so valuable to her if she could have had a mentor who understood and encouraged her. "I could always pick up the phone and talk to my family," Megan explained. "But I know there's something about having someone who thinks like you that really helps you stay on track. I think I can be that kind of support for someone younger."

I don't know about you, but when I was younger, before I discovered my strong will wasn't abnormal, I spent a lot of time being defensive about my right to have it. Even as I struggled to find myself, I secretly wondered if maybe there was something wrong with me after all. Did God approve of me even though I didn't exactly fit the "quiet, virtuous Christian woman" mold?

Fortunately, I was blessed to have a strong-willed dad who understood and brought out the best in me. Once I figured out I was okay, I spent a lot less energy being defensive and had more left over to accommodate others. But I'm not sure I would have gotten on track as soon as I did if I hadn't had someone like my dad to mentor me.

I was impressed with Megan's mature understanding of her strong will and how she could use it to encourage, challenge, and help other SWWs grow. Otherwise, who speaks into their lives? Who can understand their uniqueness?

WHY YOU'RE THE RIGHT PERSON TO MENTOR

To many of us, the idea of mentoring another SWW may seem daunting—especially if we're still trying to accept our own strong wills and keep them under control. But when we step out and share our lessons learned, we help shape and build up the leaders of other generations.

One SWW wrote about her life this way:

I want to understand me better. At this point, I hate being strong willed. I need not only correction but healing in how I see myself. I wish I were more pliable in the Potter's hand. I truly want to love and respect God and serve Him

with my whole heart. This is coming from a searching
heart that longs for breakthrough in my relationship with
God and is on a path not just to know myself better, but
more importantly to know Him.

She needs someone to help her figure out those issues, to
embrace who God made her to be. And the best person for the
job? Another SWW. Only we have been in her shoes, and better than anyone else, we can understand what she's going
through. We know how to communicate to her in a way she
can hear and accept.

Recently pastor and author Dr. Timothy Keller summed
up a great reason why it's so important for us to reach out to
other SWWs.

To be loved but not known is comforting but superficial.
To be known and not loved is our greatest fear. But to be
fully known and truly loved is a lot like being loved by
God. It is what we need more than anything. It liberates
us from pretense, humbles us out of our self-righteousness,
and fortifies us for any difficulty life can throw at us.[1]

Every young woman can benefit from having a godly
mentor, but the SWW has a distinctive need for someone who

understands her strengths and how she thinks. If you're an SWW living all out for God, you know it's not easy to keep your will centered in His. But you also know how important it is to bring your strengths and determination into line with God's purpose and plan for using them. You have a unique ability to share insights and experiences with other SWWs in ways that will resonate and encourage them without making them feel defensive.

How Can You Be the Best Mentor?

You'll find that once you decide to be open to mentoring other SWWs and you start praying that God will lead you to them, you'll find them everywhere. You know there's no specific checklist or method for figuring out how strong willed someone is. And there's no typical profile. But you can easily recognize some behaviors that stand out—especially after reading this book.

Chances are good that an SWW isn't looking for a formal mentoring program. Your approach can be as simple as a ten-minute phone call, a brisk walk or bike ride, a cup of coffee at the kitchen table or the local coffee shop. Often the best relationships are started when you affirm an SWW's strengths or accomplishments and offer encouragement and support.

Yvette Maher (see the end of chapter 5) discovered a creative and thoroughly enjoyable way to mentor many of the young women, not just the strong-willed ones, in her church:

> I began to mentor Lee, Lauren, their friends, and some of
> the young women at the ministry, in the art of food and
> the Titus verses. I was shocked to learn that some of them
> didn't purchase tomatoes because they didn't know what to
> do with them, or that they didn't use green peppers because
> they weren't sure which parts to cut out and which ones to
> leave. I showed them a potato peeler and demonstrated how
> to make stock with scraps of vegetables they had in their
> fridge. In the process, we laughed, shared our lives, and
> grew in relationship. I was able to speak into their hearts in
> a way that wouldn't have been possible in another setting.[2]

Another way to describe this whole mentoring process would be to put up some lighthouses and show land to those swimming in the uncharted ocean of possibilities. Sometimes just being present in the lives of other SWWs can reveal to them how their strong will can be used to accomplish God's purposes in their lives—and in the world.

In other words, you don't have to have formal training. Just invest time with them. Take an interest in their lives. Love them.

HOW OLD SHOULD A MENTOR BE?

There's no magical age that qualifies you to be a mentor—your experience can be far more valuable than chronological age. For example, a young adult can mentor a college student; a college student can mentor a high school student; a high school student can mentor a junior high student. The key is being able to share experiences that are relevant to the individual you're mentoring, and to do it through a biblical worldview.

Intergenerational mentoring can offer extraordinary benefits, especially when the young woman being mentored is largely surrounded only by her peer group in daily life. One woman told me she wishes she had been able to have a strong mentor when she was in college, but there were only peer counselors. She said, "I made some mistakes, and some of my worst failures were during college. I think it would have made a real difference if I'd had someone older who could have guided me. But I didn't have any natural access to those potential mentors."

You have something to offer younger SWWs. If you're presently a professional, identify a younger potential leader. If you've recently graduated from college, find a younger woman in junior high or high school. If your children are older, seek out a young mother. If you're retired, you have much to offer in any or all of the areas—spiritual, marriage, parenting, or professional. The important thing is to be willing to be used by God, and to be a messenger of His amazing love and grace.

QUICK, PRACTICAL TIPS FOR MENTORS

I gathered a few tips from several younger SWWs about what they want from a mentor. Here's what they had to say:

- Avoid being too regimented or rigid.
- Meet in a natural, comfortable setting.
- Don't lecture; share instead. If they wanted information, they'd hit the web. They are looking to you to share life experiences.
- Help them apply life knowledge to their experiences.
- Verify that something might be confidential, and if it is, keep it in the vault.
- Talk to them as a peer, but one who has more varied and extensive life experiences. In other words, don't talk down to them, as though you have life all figured out.
- Don't overshare your own problems.
- Please know what you're talking about.
- Ask more questions—give less unsolicited advice.
- Don't just try to straighten out their lives or fix their problems.

- Just because you *can* speak truth doesn't always mean you should.
- Conduct your conversations together with lots of grace.

My friend Megan told me why she has been so successful in her current relationship with the teenage girl she's mentoring. "I've been careful to keep all our conversations surrounded by grace. That way, when I have tough things to talk about with her, she can take it—because she knows more grace is coming."

You are uniquely qualified to reach out to someone, and God already has her in mind. What an incredible privilege to be trusted by Him with the responsibility of helping, in even a small way, to shape a life that's designed to change the world!

A CHALLENGE FOR THE WOMAN OF
STRENGTH AND *Purpose*

T hough this book is coming to an end, for you this is only the beginning. I believe every SWW who has committed her life to God is a woman of *strength*—with convictions of steel, standing firm in her faith even under the most relentless pressure. She is also a woman of *purpose*—with every fiber of her being dedicated to bringing honor and glory to God. Although we're diverse in almost every other respect, we are united in our desire to put Christ first in our lives and communicate His truth and love to the world.

SWWs don't always feel their strengths are welcome when it comes to participation and leadership in the church. Sometimes we may sense that our strengths are accepted more positively anywhere *but* the church. And yet we have an important role to play in the outreach and discipleship of many lost souls who are part of God's treasured creation. There are even instances when the SWW may be the only one who can reach someone who thinks as she does.

What if there are dozens of SWWs within the walls of your church who could come together in Christ to pray and fellowship and form a bond so strong that the Enemy could not defeat them? What if this group of godly SWWs could show by example how God can take the strongest will and use it for His purposes?

RAISE UP THE SWWs IN YOUR CHURCH

I was speaking to a group of more than six hundred women at a women's ministry event. Just for fun, I asked them to take my SWW quiz to find out how many scored eight points or higher. The result? Less than 25 percent. Why weren't more SWWs participating in this professionally planned and beautifully executed event? Most of the women there could name an absent friend or two who would definitely have scored high on the SWW scale. There was nothing wrong with the event itself—it just didn't have the appeal needed for more SWWs to feel compelled to come.

No one poured us out of a mold; no one can fit us into a category. I have an SWW friend who is a master gardener, bakes a mean red velvet cake, cooks like a French chef, and has a real flair for interior decorating. Another good SWW friend can't boil water, avoids eating sugar, runs every day, and still uses cement blocks for the bookshelves in her storage room. I don't fit the description of either one. Many times, SWWs have felt as though they don't belong in churches because they don't see themselves in the one-size-fits-all mold they perceive the church expects—whether or not that's true.

There are some amazing women's ministries out there. In fact, I believe many SWWs don't even realize how much some of these programs have changed as they've overcome the stereotype of being soft or fluffy. Many ministries have expanded to include topics and events that are irresistible to SWWs who are impatient to get moving, take some risks, and pick up the pace. It takes all of us, you know—the trailblazers as well as the supportive trail walkers. Is there a way you, as an SWW, can contribute to your own church's outreach?

If your church's leadership gets stuck for ideas on how to expand options for their women's programs, suggest they seek out some SWWs in the church, since it takes one to know one, and SWWs usually have no shortage of ideas.

What if we raised up an entire network of SWWs who want to live all out for God? Local churches and fellowships could reach out to this unique and largely overlooked population of women who may not have felt particularly valued in a traditional church setting before.

Here are just some of the countless benefits to banding these women together. They are able to connect and encourage one another in order to

- build up one another through the Word and help one another keep our strengths firmly grounded in Christ,
- find ways to love, respect, and honor our husbands and families,
- identify great individual strengths, even when they sometimes seem to be just irritating weaknesses,
- continually nurture and encourage new and younger SWWs, helping them discover the joy of surrendering to the One who designed them, and
- look for ways to help answer the prayers and meet the needs of others, specializing in creative and resourceful thinking to accomplish seemingly impossible tasks.

As SWWs who are called by God to be willing to do extraordinary things, attempt impossible goals, and maybe even risk everything, we need to find others who understand and share our strength and purpose. We need to mutually encourage, hold up one another in prayer, and form a bond of fellowship.

Not everyone will be a trailblazer. Not every SWW will be called to live out her life in extreme or dangerous ways. But every one of us is called to give everything we have and everything we are back to the God who created us, who knows us, who has a plan and a purpose for us.

Our obedience to God means we follow Jesus—no matter what, no matter where, no matter how. A lot of times it won't be comfortable or convenient or sometimes even tolerable. But the most important thing is *serving God.* Our strength, our purpose, lies not in the fulfillment of our own dreams but in seeking to find and do what God wants us to do.

THE NEXT STEP

It's impossible to know what the future holds—but a woman of strength and purpose is not daunted or overwhelmed when she is firmly grounded in the One who holds the future. What happens when the road to success isn't even a road? What happens if it's an almost impossible, impassable path to a destination you're not sure even exists? Sometimes obedience to God is a breathless, dangerous, heart-stopping adventure. Sometimes it's a quiet life lived intensely for the Lord. And most of the time it's something in between.

Your life is like a suspense novel that you can only read a chapter at a time—no chance to skip ahead to discover what's next or how it ends. Hold on to the one thing you *can* know for sure: God made you this way for a reason. He knows what He's doing.

I hope you feel a sense of anticipation as you finish reading this book. I'd love to hear from you—I know God is about to do some amazing things in and through your life! Please contact me at CynthiaTobias.com.

Discussion Questions

Chapter 1: Who Says I'm a Strong-Willed Woman?

1. How does our society view a woman who is described as "strong willed"? Give examples to support your answer.
2. Do you consider yourself to be a strong-willed woman (SWW)? Why or why not?
3. What are some obvious differences between an SWW with God and an SWW without God?
4. How might being an SWW be an advantage when it comes to honoring Christ?

Chapter 2: We're All Different—Yet So Alike!

1. What characteristics of an SWW do you identify with the most?
2. Describe one way in which another SWW has inspired you.
3. Think back to a time when you have seen the dark side of your strong will. How did that work out?
4. What circumstances—situation, mood, type of conversation—bring out the worst side of your strong will? The best side?

Chapter 3: Living All Out for God

1. How does Cynthia's description of repentance align with your understanding of what it means to repent? In what ways do you think SWWs sometimes misunderstand the true meaning of repentance?

2. Why might submission to God be freeing to an SWW?

3. Describe a time when God called you to obey in a small but difficult way.

4. Have you found that you're particularly aware of God's "Holy Spirit Nudges"? When have you followed an HSN and become an answer to someone else's prayer?

Chapter 4: What's Wrong with Being Self-Sufficient?

1. Do you believe self-sufficiency is a sin? Why or why not?

2. In what ways does the idea of not being in charge unsettle you? In what ways does it seem liberating?

3. When are you most tempted to "help" God figure out a situation?

4. How does a sense of self-sufficiency affect your relationship with God?

5. Describe a difficult time when God challenged you to trust Him more.

Chapter 5: Just Because You Can Doesn't Mean You Should

1. Do you ever feel you have to stay angry in order to change a situation or fight an injustice? Why or why not?

2. Describe a time when your strong will empowered you to win a battle but ultimately caused you to lose the war. (In other words, it wasn't really worth it.)

3. In what circumstances and with whom are you most likely to become impatient? Why do you think that is?

4. What is one way you could become more aware of when you're being tempted to unethically manipulate a situation?

5. What steps could you take to respond to a difficult comment or conversation with graciousness rather than anger?

Chapter 6: Directing Our Passion and Defining Our Purpose

1. Where do you most often find your joy? How does—or how could—that joy connect to the needs of other people?

2. Describe a time when God took you on a detour on the way to fulfilling your calling.

3. What vision has God given you to live out during this season of life?

4. How will you know that you are fulfilling God's purpose in your life?

Chapter 7: Leadership with Integrity

1. What words or phrases would you use to describe Christ-like leadership?
2. In what areas do you serve as a leader right now?
3. Do you have any partners who hold you accountable in your words and actions? If not, identify one or two individuals who might be able to serve you in this way.
4. What would it look like for you to let Christ guide you in your leadership roles?

Chapter 8: Strong-Willed Women and the Men Who Love Them

1. In what ways is your strong will a gift in your marriage? In what ways might it be a hindrance?
2. How do your strengths and your husband's strengths complement each other?
3. Were you surprised to learn that most couples experience conflict on a near-daily basis? Why or why not? Do you find that encouraging or discouraging? Why?
4. In what ways have you seen conflict bring you and your spouse closer together?

Chapter 9: Moms and Kids Who Share Strong Will

1. How does being an SWW affect your parenting style?
2. What do you find most challenging about parenting a strong-willed child?
3. What gifts do you see in your child that come from her strong will? How could you use those gifts to help your child see his personality in a more positive light?
4. Identify one thing you could do this week to deepen your relationship with your strong-willed child.

Chapter 10: Mentoring the Next Generation

1. Why is it important for an SWW to have a mentor and be a mentor?
2. When have you been able to learn from an older or wiser SWW? In what way was that relationship (or conversation or book) helpful to you?
3. Who is an SWW you could mentor? What is one step you could take this week toward building that mentoring relationship?

Chapter 11: A Challenge for the Woman of Strength and Purpose

1. Do you feel your strengths as an SWW are welcomed in your church? Explain your answer.

2. How might you be able to raise up other SWWs in your church to strengthen your faith community?

3. In what ways has reading this book changed your view of yourself as an SWW?

4. Cynthia writes, "Our strength, our purpose, lies not in the fulfillment of our own dreams but in seeking to find and do what God wants us to do." What is the next step you will take to further your search for God's purpose in your life? How can you direct your strong will to help you better serve God today?

Acknowledgments

I owe a great debt of gratitude to so many! I want to recognize and thank my all-star editor and friend, Gwen Ellis, for her patience and encouragement as she went above and beyond her job description on the original manuscript. I also want to thank Ginger Kolbaba, my other editor, who refined and challenged me to make this the best book I could. I am especially grateful to my husband, Jack Talley, who put up with my spending a lot of time away in order to write—as well as a certain amount of grouchiness that comes with the pressure of deadlines. A special thanks goes to my strong-willed millennial friends, like Megan Reed Hansen and others, who shared their hearts and insights into their generation. It's always a privilege to work with the professionals at WaterBrook, an organization that truly lifts up Christ in word and deed. Most of all, I want to give a heartfelt thank-you to the hundreds of strong-willed women all over the world who took my surveys and gave me priceless advice and comments.

This book would not have been possible without the *true* Writer, God, who was with me every step of the way. It is my sincere prayer that everything I say and do will bring glory to Him.

Notes

Chapter 3: Living All Out for God

1. Liz Curtis Higgs, *Rise and Shine* (Colorado Springs: WaterBrook, 2002), 15.

2. Eugene Peterson, *A Long Obedience in the Same Direction* (Downers Grove, IL: InterVarsity, 2000), 29–30.

3. C. S. Lewis, *Mere Christianity* (San Francisco: HarperOne, 2001), 57.

4 Rick Warren, *The Purpose Driven Life* (Grand Rapids, MI: Zondervan, 2012), 82.

5. Alison Dellenbaugh, "When Your Calling Feels Too Small," *Gifted for Leadership* (blog), *Christianity Today*, May 29, 2014, www.christianitytoday.com/gifted-for-leadership/2014/may/when-your-calling-feels-too-small.html.

6. David McCasland, *Oswald Chambers: Abandoned to God* (Grand Rapids, MI: Discovery House, 1998), 109.

Chapter 4: What's Wrong with Being Self-Sufficient?

1. Oswald Chambers, *My Utmost for His Highest, Classic Edition* (Ulrichsville, OH: Barbour, 2015), July 4, 186.

Chapter 5: Just Because You Can Doesn't Mean You Should

1. Roma Downey, from her survey response, March 22, 2014.
2. Yvette Maher, *My Hair and God's Mercies* (Colorado Springs: Focus on the Family, 2012), Kindle edition.
3. Yvette Maher, *My Hair and God's Mercies*.

Chapter 6: Directing Our Passion and Defining Our Purpose

1. Brennan Manning, *The Signature of Jesus* (Colorado Springs: Multnomah, 1996), 14.
2. Oswald Chambers, *My Utmost for His Highest, Classic Edition* (Ulrichsville, OH: Barbour, 2015), January 2, 2.
3. Oswald Chambers, *My Utmost for His Highest*, January 4, 4.
4. See Isaiah 55:8–9.
5. Larry Crabb, quoted in *The Family Project: A Divine Reflection*, "Session 6: What God Has Joined To-gether" (Colorado Springs: Focus on the Family, 2014), DVD.
6. Jan Wismer, "Celebrating Elisabeth Elliot's Life: A Pioneer and Prayer Warrior," *Today's Christian Woman*, October 2013, www.todayschristianwoman.com/articles/2013/october/elisabeth-elliot-pioneer-and-prayer-warrior

.html?start=3. Also, Elisabeth was referring to Deuter-onomy 33:27: "The eternal God is thy refuge, and underneath are the everlasting arms" (KJV).

7. Lynne Hybels, "Evangelicals and Gender Equality," *lynnehybels* (blog), November 18, 2013, www.lynne hybels.com/evangelicals-and-gender-equality.

8. Janine tells more of her story in her two books, *It's Not Okay with Me* and *Is It Okay with You?* It's an amazing story of a woman of faith, courage, and determination who had to do something to make a difference in the world.

Chapter 7: Leadership with Integrity

1. John Stott, *Issues Facing Christians Today,* 4th ed. (Grand Rapids, MI: Zondervan, 2006), 494.

2. Lois P. Frankel and Carol Frohlinger, *Nice Girls Just Don't Get It* (New York: Harmony, 2011), 87.

3. Selena Rezvani, *Pushback* (San Francisco: Jossey-Bass, 2012), xiii, and Sheila Murphy, quoted in the same, 44.

4. Nancy Beach, *Gifted to Lead* (Grand Rapids, MI: Zondervan, 2008), 50.

5. Tony Schwartz, "What Women Know About Leadership That Men Don't," *Harvard Business Review,* October 30, 2012, https://hbr.org/2012/10/what-women-know-that -men-dont.

6. Lori Wilhite and Brandi Wilson, *Leading and Loving It* (Nashville: FaithWords, 2013), Kindle edition.

Chapter 8: Strong-Willed Women and the Men Who Love Them

1. See Proverbs 27:17.
2. Les Parrott and Leslie Parrott, *The Good Fight* (Brentwood, TN: Worthy, 2013), 1.
3. Parrott and Parrott, *The Good Fight*, 2–3.

Chapter 9: Moms and Kids Who Share Strong Will

1. *Parenting with Love and Logic* is an excellent resource by Foster Cline, MD, and Jim Fay.
2. Rob Parsons, *Bringing Home the Prodigals* (Colorado Springs: Authentic, 2008), 6–7.
3. Cynthia Ulrich Tobias, *You Can't Make Me!* (Colorado Springs: WaterBrook, 2012), 2–3.

Chapter 10: Mentoring the Next Generation

1. Dr. Timothy Keller, Facebook post, January 14, 2016, www.facebook.com/search/top/?q=timothy%20keller.
2. Yvette Maher, *My Hair and God's Mercies* (Colorado Springs: Focus on the Family, 2012), Kindle edition.

DISCOVER POSITIVE WAYS TO APPROACH AND MOTIVATE YOUR STRONG-WILLED CHILD

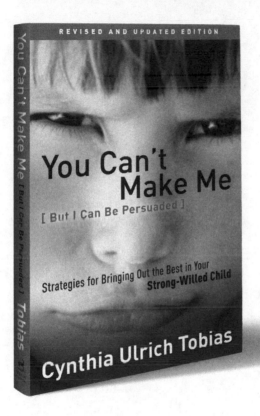

Bring peace to your family, heal your relationship with your strong-willed child, and face the challenge of disciplining and directing a stubborn will without breaking your child's spirit.

WATERBROOK

www.waterbrookmultnomah.com